THE LAST TEMPTATION OF HOLLYWOOD

Larry W. Poland, Ph.D.

Mastermedia International, Inc.
2102 Palm Avenue
Highland, California 92346

The Last Temptation of Hollywood
Copyright © 1988 by Larry W. Poland, Ph. D.

Unless otherwise noted, Scripture references are taken from the Holy Bible: New International Version (North American Edition), copyright © 1973, 1978, 1984 by the International Bible Society. Used by permission of Zondervan Bible Publishers.

Library of Congress Catalog Card Number: 88-63214

ISBN 0-9621692-0-X

First Edition, Second Printing (June 1989)

MASTERMEDIA INTERNATIONAL, INC., 2102 Palm Avenue, Highland, CA 92346

Printed in the United States of America

Dedication

This book is dedicated to the deeply committed
Christians who are working professionals in film and
television, those who have to "work out their beliefs"
in an environment that is often hostile to religious
faith in general and to a personal commitment to
Jesus Christ in particular.

It is hoped that God will provide each media believer
with the wisdom and power to resolve the dynamic
tensions between loyalty to God and the human
authority structure, between obedience to the
commands of Scripture and involvement in the media
subculture, and between a strong expression of
personal values and respect
for the varying beliefs of others.

It is also hoped that the positive moral influence
of these dedicated professionals
will have a significant impact
on the moral content of media in the decades to come --
both in *restraining* the flood of impurity
and irresponsibility and in
creating media products
which elevate the human spirit.

Contents

Introduction

I'm not sure whether they are weaker moments or stronger, those brief spans of time when I desire to be able to see and know the future. As I pursue my "on-one-hand" and "on-the-other-hand" dialogues, I am often torn between being desperate to know what's ahead and being mighty grateful to God that I don't.

At points I have wished I could have seen what would happen when Tim Penland, my film marketing friend, asked me to consult with him on the project with Universal Pictures called *The Last Temptation of Christ*. I deeply desired to know how all of this would turn out, what cosmic purpose would be served by my involvement, and what eternal "trade offs" would declare this a good investment of my time and effort or a colossal waste.

At other points I have been quite thankful that I could not see ahead. While I might have been game for some of the experience and character construction to be derived from a central position in the *Last Temptation* flap, I most likely would have been too chicken to pursue it. I probably would have desired the diploma without having to take the courses and pass the finals.

But, in the divine scheme of things, I never had a choice. I ended up in the eye of this international tornado, blown by a series of seemingly innocent little gusts, winds which no one could have predicted would land me with such turbulence where I am --writing a book on this century's most passionate conflict between Christians and Hollywood.

I am a reluctant author. I don't write this book for personal gain. In very real terms this book already has cost me more, in more ways, than I can afford. And the billing isn't all in.

I don't write this out of self-defense or vengeance. My world view is so deeply rooted in the concept that "God keeps good books" that I have no personal ledgers to balance.

I am not writing for some noble sounding "a-man-has-gotta-do-what-a-man-has-gotta-do" motivation, either. But I am writing because I feel I am under constraint to do so by a moral imperative.

If this book had not been written, a number of major voids would exist in this nation:

*   The vast majority of the American people --wonderful, fair-minded people--would not have access to the truth behind the distorted and superficial news stories they received about *The Last Temptation*, truth which is crucial to their understanding of major forces at work in our land.

*   The motivations and machinations of one of this country's most powerful corporations would never have been uncovered, enabling that company to *avoid public accountability* for decisions which resulted in the production and release of this movie and may well result in similar destructive decisions in the future.

* No alarm would be sounded about the brazen attacks against religious faith in America represented both by the film in question and by the actions of the men and women responsible for foisting it on the global public.

* A major movie studio's entry into religious propaganda with a film pitching New Age thinking would not have been revealed-- thinking apparently espoused so deeply by some at Universal Pictures that they risked major financial loss and decades of destructive public relations to spread it.

* A decade from now, when those of deep religious--especially Christian--convictions are experiencing increasing persecution, someone might dare to point the just finger of accusation at me and say, "You knew this was going on! You knew what was happening before it got this bad! Why didn't you do something to warn us? How can you justify not doing something to stop it?"

As you read this, do not get caught up in the incidents, the details, or the emotions of the story. Think *lessons* --what can we learn from this? Think *morals*--what are the morals of this story? Think *strategy*--what is the game plan of the enemies of faith? What are the defensive and offensive strategies used to respond to them?

Finally, think *response*--what call to vigilance, to action, does this story sound? For, if you think this matter is over now that the film is released and the studio has lost millions on its decision, think again! Knowing the film was dead at the box office, Universal Pictures had 200,000 eight page, full color "study guides" printed for use with the film by schools, churches, and other institutions! They were willing to put "good money after bad" to get the film's twisted, religious message out--all without identifying themselves on the publication!

You hold in your hands a prophetic message. It is flawed and imperfect. In places it may fall prey to some of the dynamics it decries. Despite attempts to be balanced and accurate, I have written only *one side* of the story, the *untold* side. Understand this as you read! If you want the *told* side, the periodical section of your local library is filled with it.

Don't miss the prophecy. The message is: *"If you do not awaken and stir this society with a passionate declaration and defense of Judeo-Christian values, you will have no basis to complain when you are enslaved by those with contempt for those values."*

It is the Gresham's Law of a republic: *Dear values which are left undefended will inevitably be driven out by cheap values which are.*

1

Approaching the Chasm

Leave it to New York traffic.

Here I was in the office of an aging, off-Broadway high rise with a varied assemblage of people I didn't know, in a business I didn't understand, to talk about a Broadway show I knew nothing about, in a meeting I hadn't called! If only my friend, Tim Penland, who had gotten me into this, would show up to rescue me! But Tim had called saying that he was hung up in traffic in a Yellow Cab and wouldn't arrive for a while. Nice guy!

I knew nothing about marketing show biz product. That was Tim's specialty. He was the guy who had shared the success of marketing *Chariots of Fire* and *The Mission* to Christian structures across America. Tim was the man who had been called in by a top Broadway show producer to explore the possibility of marketing a new musical, *King*, to Christians in and around New York. Tim had asked me to accompany him because I had been doing consulting and research for him on the Christian marketplace.

Evangelical Christians were my specialty. I was one, had grown up with them, understood them, could call most of their leaders on a first name basis, could talk their language, and, with my Ph. D. in social science, knew how to analyze them.

Right now I was stuck in a ten by ten office decorated with Broadway show posters, stacks of scripts and

9

papers, personal artifacts, and five people who wanted to make money and gain notability through a musical on the life of Martin Luther King. There was The Producer, a highly successful, young, Jewish man with shoulder length hair and casual clothes, who peered over the stratified clutter on his desk trying to figure what I was doing in a pin-striped suit. There was an attactive black woman who had a mischievous sparkle in her eyes and a touch of cynicism in her speech and demeanor. There was The Musician, a larger Jewish man who seemed pretty much in charge of the meeting even though he sat on the sofa instead of behind the desk. There was a beautifully poised anglo lady with jet black hair and dark eyes whose quietness couldn't hide her intelligence. Then there was The Writer. He was a well groomed, distinguished looking man past mid-life with major successes like *Ghandi* and *Cry Freedom* on his resume. *King* was his latest creative effort.

Without anyone calling it to order, banging a gavel, or saying an invocation, the meeting began. All eyes were on me and the empty chair where the convener of this meeting was supposed to be sitting.

"Tell us about your work marketing films?" was the first query.

"Well, you see, that is Mr. Penland's business. I am just a consultant with Penland Productions." There was an awkward pause which seemed to say, "Are we wasting our time with this guy or what?"

"What kind of consulting do you do for Mr. Penland?" was question two.

"I consult with him in the marketing of films to

10

Christians, particularly evangelical Christians." I was feeling a little more comfortable now that the subject was one I could handle. There was no hostility in the room, but nobody pointing to a cross on his neck chain either.

"*Evangelical* Christians? What does that mean?"

Can you believe New Yorker bluntness? In three questions they were into my soul!

"*Evangelicals* are Christians who endeavor to share good news--that's what "evangelical" means--the "good news" of forgiveness through Jesus Christ. They also profess to have had a born again experience with Jesus Christ. George Gallup says there are 82.5 million of them in America."[1] They looked shocked and intrigued. I continued, "They represent an incredible market that is hidden to most entertainment people."

"How do they differ from the rest of the country?" They were showing more cautious interest.

"Widely." I came back. "They have their own subculture, maintain a network of over a thousand radio stations and three hundred TV stations, are in a tight infrastructure of churches and denominations, have very well defined and deeply held values, and even have their own language?"

"What? You're kidding!" They were obviously quite intrigued.

"No, seriously. I call it Christianese."

The lady with the mischievous sparkle in her eyes

jumped in as if to call my bluff. "Give us some examples." she challenged.

"Okay," I responded, knowing I was playing a game I could win. "Anybody here know what the phrase 'under the blood' means?"

They looked at each other like they thought I was playing dirty. After a sufficient period of silence to establish that I didn't have any takers, I went on.

"Under Old Testament Jewish law when there was to be a ceremony of atonement for sin, the priest had to kill a lamb and sprinkle the blood around the sacrifice to satisfy God's requirements. When John the Baptist introduced Jesus, he declared, 'Behold the lamb of God who takes away the sin of the world.' We Christians believe that the reason Christ had to shed his blood was to atone for our wrongdoing. So when we go to God for forgiveness and receive it, we say, 'Well, that sin is *under the blood'*."

A few restrained "aha's" circled the room, and the "sparkle lady" came back for more. "What are some other examples?"

I was giving a short primer on "sanctified" and "justified" when the door flung open and Tim breathlessly strode in, apologizing for the taxicab ordeal that made him late. Being New Yorkers, they understood.

As the discussion of the marketing of *King* proceeded, I assumed the role for which I was chosen in this meeting, quiet support to the expert. At one point Tim indicated strong agreement with a resonant and hearty

Oklahoma "Aaamen," and the mischievous lady looked at me if as to say, "I think I'm hearing your language." Later Tim referred to his work overload as having more work than he could "say Grace over." This time the lady's alert glance and raised eyebrow telegraphed, "Could this be Christianese?" I gave her an affirmative nod, and she smiled proudly.

In my "free mind time," while others were carrying the weight of the conversation, I kept going back to that interaction about evangelical Christians. I realized I could have been describing *Martians* to these people. They didn't have a *clue* about evangelicals.

There was an enormous information gap, a cultural chasm, between us. It was troubling to me. It's no wonder, I thought, that media people throw around "Jesus Christ" as swear words. They don't know that what they are doing is as offensive to us as using "nigger" is to a black person. They really do not know.

It's not that I had not peered across this chasm before. In eight and a half years of working with leaders in media in Hollywood, I had seen it often. It had surfaced in my interactions with top producers and executives. It surfaced at a Television Academy conference on teenage pregnancy when I stood to suggest, however mildly, that an alternative to condoms in school colors would be for teenagers to seek counsel from parents or ministers. I was loudly denounced by a lady on NBC's staff sitting in front of me. We obviously were from different worlds, from opposite sides of a great canyon separating media people from Christians.

With Tim it was different. Ever since Tim had joined the Key Man group which I lead for Christian executives, producers, and directors in Hollywood, Tim and I had known we were kindred spirits. As I worked with this group of powerful men, I had observed Tim to be a gentle giant and without guile. His slight, Oklahoma accent and his Bible belt lingo belied his good business head and his knowledge of the film industry. Tim didn't seem to "fit" in Hollywood with it's tell-'em-whatever-they-want-to-hear patter and the underlying obsession with vanity. Tim said he had been "led" to Hollywood, and nobody doubted it. It was obvious that he was enough "out of phase" with Hollyweird that if God hadn't brought him, he wouldn't be here.

Even though I noticed some cross cultural awkwardness on occasions when Tim would punctuate the Key Man meetings with his throaty, camp meeting "Aaaaaamen," none of the network or production company execs in the group questioned Tim's sincerity. We had all heard how Tim had "backslidden" from the Christian faith of his youth, and had become an alcoholic. Tim had told us of wandering into a church meeting and of having some lovely older ladies pray over him at decision time. Tim would pause and tell us how God "worked a miracle" in him, how he "hadn't had a drink since," and how God gave him a fine Christian wife and a new start in life. Nobody doubted the story, even if it did sound an awful lot like some of those hokey "gospel" films that have circulated around the country for decades. Tim was telling the truth. As a Christian Tim was a "hundred percenter."

I must admit I wasn't ready for the next chapter in Tim's business life. Around the turn of the year Tim had been contacted by Tom Pollock, Si Kornblitt, and Sally Van Slyke, three top executives at Universal

14

Pictures. They had heard of his work on *Chariots* and *Mission* and said they really needed his help on another film that they knew was facing problems. Sally said the film was facing, not a *million* dollar problem but potentially a *billion* dollar problem." It was a Martin Scorsese film about Christ.

As Tim told me of his conversation with Universal, my mind raced back to a short squib I had read in Donald Wildmon's American Family Association publication. I dug it out. There it was, a four or five paragraph article declaring that Universal Pictures was reviving a project that Paramount had dropped in 1983, a film based on Nikos Kazantzakis' book, *The Last Temptation of Christ*. The article described the novel as blasphemous, as portraying Christ as a wimpy, lust driven character who, in a dream sequence, marries and has sex with Mary Magdalene, marries Mary of Bethany, commits adultery with her sister, Martha, and has children by both. I shared this information with Tim.

"I am familiar with the book, Larry," Tim said, "But Tom Pollock assured me that Universal has no intention of releasing a blasphemous film. He poured out his heart to me. They really want me to work on this film. What do I do?"

"Tim, you wouldn't be able to work on a film that attacks the character of Christ, would you?"

"Of course not. I could never support a film that defames my Lord. But I really don't know much about it. Sally is trying to set up a meeting with Tom Pollock to discuss the possibility of my working on the film with them. I guess I'll find out more if that meeting

15

comes off."

The meeting did come off in early January. Tim was ushered in royal style through the deep carpet area of Universal's executive suite to a brightly lit room that was not so rich in appointments as the wealth of the corporation might allow. Gathered there were Sally Van Slyke, head of publicity, Sean Daniel, head of world wide production, Si Kornblitt, head of marketing, and The Man, Tom Pollock, Universal's chairman of the board. Tim's mindset going into the meeting was that he was making a presentation, a "pitch" as it is called in the business. As he lowered his large frame into an uncomfortably overstuffed sofa and the meeting began, Tim discovered *he was being pitched.*

The Man began to speak. He sketched the history of the project and of its development with Scorsese. Tom evidenced that he had thoroughly researched all aspects of the film. While neither he nor anyone else in leadership at Universal had seen the film at that point, he communicated awareness of the more intimate thoughts of Scorsese on the project. His eloquence and mental sharpness reflected a man who had not gotten to his position by nepotism or some fluke of organizational dynamics.

As Tom Pollock spoke, he became more and more impassioned. He indicated that Universal was concerned about the increasing number of critical calls and letters that were beginning to fill the mailroom. "Tim," he declared, "it is *not* our desire to release a film defaming Christ," More than once he said, "This is going to be a faith affirming film. Martin has assured us of that. We *need your help* in working with

16

Christians." Now he was speaking like an evangelist, like Billy Graham promoting a deeply spiritual film to a contingent of potential investors. He ended by saying, " . . . I say all of this, and I am a Jew!"

Not a little breathless by the presentation, Tim responded, "Well, I don't know if I can help you, but I am willing to try. Let me see what I can do. I do think that you need to set up screenings with religious leaders as soon as possible to get a feel for what kind of challenges you face."

"Consider it done, Tim!" Tom said.

Tim left the room with his head orbiting. He had never had this kind of interchange with the powerful head of a major studio in his entire career. He had never been pursued like this; he was accustomed to pursuing. Pollock's earnestness was the thing that impressed him. If Pollock were only half so much in need of Tim's help as he indicated, how could he turn his back on him?

There was no talk of money. Pollock didn't ask about nor suggest remuneration. Tim didn't ask for nor expect any. This was a person with a need that Tim might be able to fill. Tim responded with characteristic generosity, willing to serve without thinking of money.

Tim called me with a report on the meeting. "Larry, I have never seen anyone more earnest than Tom Pollock. He really sold me. He thinks this film may even be one that could be marketed to the Christian community. He says Martin Scorsese has assured Universal that this will be a 'faith affirming' film. The world could use a

17

film about Christ that dealt realistically with His humanity without denying His deity."

"Tim, if it is a faith affirming film, it will surely bear little resemblance to the book, from what I've heard."

"Yes, but you know how directors take liberties with novels. Besides, wouldn't it be great if God could use us to build some bridges between the Christian community and the biggest film company in Hollywood?"

"Now that *is* appealing to me, Tim. There is such an enormous chasm between Hollywood and the Christians that it really would be great if we could establish a trust relationship with one of the major studios. That could set the precedent for building other bridges. But we need to be careful. We constantly need to calculate the downsides of such a relationship."

"Naturally. The biggest downside would be if Universal execs were seeking to use us in some way, exploiting us for their own purposes."

I agreed, and Tim tiptoed into his relationship with the three amigos from Universal. His efforts were already beginning to help their situation by the end of the first two weeks of *gratis* service for them. They were impressed. They were particularly stunned by Donald Wildmon's willingness to hold off his first, major, direct mail barrage after Tim had talked to him. They raised the subject of a more formal consulting relationship, of paying Tim for his efforts.

"Larry," Tim said, they want me to enter into a paid consulting relationship with them." And if I go into a more formal relationship, I would want you to go into it

18

with me. I need some spiritual accountability, and I need your knowledge of the Christian leaders across the country."

"Hey, man, you know I am ready to help you in any way I can. But time is my most scarce commodity. I have a big family, a growing, young church to shepherd, and a ministry in Hollywood and New York to oversee. The last thing I need is to be a film consultant!"

"I wouldn't want you to do it for nothing, Larry. If Universal pays me, I would certainly want to pay you for what you would do on the project."

"Tim, the money is no inducement. My time is more important to me than the money. Look, let me pray about it and see if I think God wants me to help out. If I do, it will be because of my love for you as a brother and because I can see the great potential of building bridges between Hollywood and the Christians. Even then, any time would have to come out of evenings or days off, time that isn't already dedicated to my vocational priorities."

"Fine, pray about it, Larry. But this could be a great opportunity to influence a film and build some trust. I have already told Universal that if this film is blasphemous or if the Christian community views it as destructive, I will resign and grab a picket sign the minute I discover it. They know that a number of Christian organizations are beginning to mount protests. They have already received enough cards and letters to convince them of that."

The Key Men were enlisted to pray for Tim's decision. Most were pretty positive about the possibilities--all except one who had been in the film business for years. "You have to watch 'em, Tim. They may be just planning to use you," he said more than once.

I gave a lot of thought and prayer to my response to work with Tim, and it all came together. I drafted a plan for a working relationship and sent it to Tim. I felt comfortable with the plan in part because I perceived it as short term. This was early January, and Universal said it was planning to release the film to theaters in early October. I figured we would know where we stood on the film in a matter of weeks.

As I thought through where Tim was with Universal, I figured I might be able to help him impress the studio executives. Drawing on my doctoral experience in social science research, I drafted a six page paper titled, "The Christian Community Market: A Profile with Implications for Film and Television Industries." I presented data on American Christians on the stated premise that "Every successful company must know its potential markets" and "Seldom have entertainment industries factored in a distinctive and numerically large body of Americans known as the Christian community."

In that document, which Tim passed on to Universal's leadership, I observed that 86% of Americans view themselves as "Christian" with 59% of those calling themselves protestants and 27% Catholics.[2] I pointed out that of these 215 million Christians 61.7% or 132.6 million were "non-evangelicals" and 38.3% or 82.5 million viewed themselves as "evangelicals."[3]

In describing the evangelicals, I noted that these are people who claim they have had a "born again" exper-

20

ience with Jesus Christ. They are twice as likely as non-evangelicals to say that their faith is "very important" to them. They are three times as likely to be concerned with "the moral and religious decline of America."[4]

At the same time, I noted that Christians are media consumers. More than the national average, 96% watch television daily. Their favorite programs are news (55%), sports (26%), and feature movies (23%). I also relayed that 54.2% attend one or more movies a year.[5]

In a final few paragraphs that seemed eerily prophetic later, I indicated that the Christian marketplace was "a force to reckon with in public relations strategies." I reminded Universal that Christians had been able to get *Playboy* and *Penthouse* pulled from Seven Eleven stores nationwide, that they were in a boycott against Holiday Inns for showing cable porn in rooms, and that they had raised such a stink with CBS that the network had been forced to cancel its scheduled "Garbage Pail Kids" children's series. I also indicated to them that a quick survey of Christian leaders indicated that a number were planning to mount a protest against the movie version of *The Last Temptation of Christ.*

Did Tom Pollock, Universal Pictures' chairman, read my paper? Did he digest it? Did he read it and calculate that this "faith affirming film" could be a hit with Christians? Did he read it and decide the protest of Christians could swell the box office of a controversial film? Only Mr. Pollock can say for sure.

Tim continued to weigh the proposal for a working relationship. Tim liked Pollock, Kornblitt, and Van

Slyke. He liked the idea of working together with them. He liked the idea of working with Universal. He liked the idea of trying to build relationships between the Christians and Hollywood. He liked the idea of doing some high level business for Penland Productions, if he didn't have to sell his soul to do it. He had the peace of God about his decision, so he summarized his willingness to help in a letter to Universal. They responded promptly.

"Well, it's settled, Larry. I have committed to help Universal manage its relationships with the Christian community. If the film is suitable for marketing to Christians, we'll do that. If it isn't, I'll quit. But until we know for sure, I'll do the best I can to earn my money."

With this simple agreement a cable was stretched across the chasm between Hollywood and the Christians. This chasm once was so wide that some Christians viewed all films and movie houses as "tools of the devil." Many believers today who would enjoy many of Tinseltown's cinema tales have been put off by that one, inevitable, sleazy sex scene or the predictable trashy language. Despite some rapprochement in the fifties and sixties, this gulf has widened in the last quarter of a century. Screenland has been perceived as purposely attacking the traditional family, marital fidelity, Judeo-Christian morality, and faith. Hopefully this new cable would soon expand into girders, trusses, and a bridge strong enough to carry those on both sides of the gorge into a new era of communication and trust.

2

Bridge Building

It was a grand dream, building bridges between Hollywood and the Christian community. With the passing of the old days of the movie "censor board," which was peopled by diverse members of the religious community, there has been no structured relationship between faith and films. Most clergymen agree that since the advent of the Motion Picture Association of America and the movie ratings system there has been precious little moral and no measurable religious impact on film makers. It is consensus that with Jack Valenti in the saddle as the head of the MPAA, the filmmakers have been policing themselves. In another manner of speaking, the foxes have been guarding the chickens.

I got involved in the "circular reasoning" on Hollywood's moral climate early in my research into the spiritual dynamics of film and television. In the six months that I met with leaders of the industry to find out "the extent to which personal faith affects the lives and decisions of the movers and shakers in Hollywood" I got the line that "films and TV don't *influence* the values of the American people, they only *reflect* the values of the populace." I was told flatly by a vice president for public relations of one the major networks that his network had no accountability for the network's programming. He asserted that the control lay fully in the hands of those who turned the knobs on TV sets. "We just provide what people want, and what they want is determined by how many knobs are 'on'."

I countered that there were a finite number of programs to choose from on TV in the same way that there are a finite number of items on a grocer's shelves. While it is true that a grocery shopper makes decisions as to what he drops in his basket as he roams the aisles, it must be remembered that the grocer *stocks the shelves.* If he puts cocaine on the shelves, he cannot blame the resulting drug addiction totally on shoppers, even if he can prove the addiction is good for his business. There is some moral accountability for what both grocers and film and TV producers "put on the shelves!"

In the same way, it seems to me, the absence of any kind of structured communication or relationship between the religious community and the filmmakers is a setup for what has happened to the moral character of Hollywood product in the last twenty five years. It helps explain why, by the industry's own ratings, only 2.3% of films in a recent year were rated "G" and why 76% were rated "R" or "PG-13."[6] There is no moral accountability or structured communication between religious leaders, who traditionally have been the guardians of the public morals, and movie moguls. And research into the personal values of media's leadership, especially that done by Lichter, Lichter, and Rothman, provides dramatic evidence that Hollywood isn't likely to lead America's values any direction but down.

That was what made the possibility of working with Universal Pictures so seductive. If, for the first time in decades, a major studio could establish trust relationships, bridges across the vast chasm of suspicion and contempt that separates Hollywood from the Christian community, think of the possibilities!

Without any hideous governmental intervention called "regulation" or "censorship" or any religious approval board in Hollywood it might be possible for movie makers to rise to a level of accountability based on mutual good will. "Building bridges to the Christian community" was exactly what Si Kornblitt told one Scott Dugan of *The Hollywood Reporter* that Tim would be doing.[7]

That was exactly what Pope John Paul II declared to be the vision when he addressed hundreds of Hollywood's most powerful figures on September 15, 1987:

> Your profession subjects you to a great measure of accountability--accountability to God, to the community, and before the witness of history . . . . The proper exercise of the right of information demands that the content of what is communicated be true . . . . Included here is the obligation to avoid any manipulation of truth for any reason . . . . The confidence that the community has in you honors you deeply and challenges you mightily. Your work can be a force for great good or great evil . . . . You have untold possibilities for good, ominous possibilities for destruction. It is the difference between . . . death or life of the spirit. And it is a matter of choice . . . . The church stands ready to help you by her encouragement and to support you in all your worthy aims.[8]

On that occasion the pope had been introduced by a man commonly recognized to be the most powerful man in media, a man who sat with moist eyes during the remarks of this moral and spiritual representative of

800 million Catholic believers worldwide--Lew Wasserman, Chairman of MCA/Universal. If the dream could not be realized in Lew's company, in which major studio *could* it be realized?

Things were going well for Tim Penland at "The Black Tower," MCA/ Universal's black glassed, high rise headquarters in Universal City, California. From competent, high control, chairman Tom Pollock to dynamic, spiritually sensitive Sally Van Slyke, things were a poppin'. Tim was establishing very open communication with Tom, Si, and Sally. They seemed to be approaching the new relationship with enthusiasm. Even given the stacks of pink telephone message slips the three received each day, Tim had no problem getting return calls.

There was talk of inviting ministers to screenings of the film, of taking out full page ads in Christian periodicals, and of making statements at major gatherings of believers nationwide. Tim and I had strategized that one of the most influential gatherings of evangelical representatives in America would take place in Washington in a few days, the National Religious Broadcasters convention. In my paper I had told Universal that evangelicals had 1393 radio stations across America, 259 television stations, plus a host of cable, direct broadcast, and production entities. Tim and I knew that they would all be represented at NRB. It seemed that this was the first major place to "spread the word" of Universal's desire to work with Christians on its new, though potentially controversial, Christ film.

But even before the convention of broadcasters, Tim was busy presenting possible strategies to Universal and contacting Christian leaders. Universal was excited about a strategy of inviting ministers across the nation to pre-screenings of the film, ostensibly to make them salespersons with their own congregations and spheres of influence. In its grandest form this approach would make sure that ministers were provided with free admission to a theater in their own geographical areas. It was suggested that an entire ministerial mailing list of 180,000 be given this invitation!

I drafted a letter for Universal executives to send out to the ministers. With minor edits the letter was viewed as acceptable, some even thought "brilliant," in its appeal to ministers to hold their fire in a spirit of good faith until the film could be seen. Included was an excerpt from a statement by Martin Scorsese assuring the ministers that the film would depict Jesus "as sinless, as deity, and as the savior of mankind."

Armed with this kind of statement and encouraged by the tremendous support we were getting from Pollock, Kornblitt, and Van Slyke, Tim and I headed east for the National Religious Broadcasters convention. I already had Mastermedia business in New York, so it worked out well for the two us us to hit both New York and Washington. In New York we talked with some Broadway show producers and had an appointment with an Orion Pictures representative on the possibility of getting Christians involved in promoting the film, *Dominic and Eugene.* Then we flew into Washington, D.C., full of confidence and anticipation.

D. Barry Reardon, President of Warner Brothers Distribution, David Putnam, producer of both *Chariots of Fire* and *The Mission*, and Ken Wales, producer of Billy Graham's *The Prodigal*, were to receive special awards at the convention. Tim was scheduled to make a statement on behalf of Universal to the delegates at that same session. It was expected that it would be a highlight of the convention.

Tim and I were rooming together. The day or so before the announcement was filled with lengthy calls between the Black Tower and our hotel room. I had prepared and Tim had edited a written statement to be delivered and distributed at NRB. Black Tower executives went over and over the statement, changing wording, debating whose name should go at the bottom of the statement, and generally rehashing the matter. Obviously, this was a significant matter to Tom Pollock and company. They made it clear, finally, that they did not want a written statement handed out. They just wanted Tim to speak for Universal without any specific name being tagged to his "remarks."

I didn't understand this. If you want to be sure you are quoted accurately, you prepare a written statement, deliver it from your manuscript, then hand out copies of the manuscript. It seemed strange to me at the time that, if the statement was such a big deal that they spent all that time and money on conference calls to our hotel, they didn't want one of their names on it, didn't want Tim to deliver a written statement, and didn't want one handed out. We had no reason to think they might not want a hard and fast record of their statement to the Christian broadcasters.

Over a long, private lunch the day of the presentation a half dozen of us had very meaningful interaction at the table at which Reardon and Putnam served as unofficial honored guests. Barry Reardon expressed his desire that Christians would get behind films like *The*

28

Mission, and noted that Christians can't expect studios to produce more films they like if they don't support the ones they do produce." David Putnam reflected on his brief tenure as president of Columbia Pictures, on the exorbitant, rising costs of making major motion pictures, and on the ethics and moral character of the film business. He had just gotten off the plane from a Moscow film conclave and was obviously stirred by the impressions he had received from Soviet filmmakers in contrast to his experiences with American ones. In a discussion of what film content offends Christians, I remember suggesting that "to release a film attacking Christ in America makes about as much sense as releasing a film in Teheran defaming Mohammed." We had a good chuckle, and the point was not lost.

The presentation at a mid-afternoon session of NRB was poorly attended and was interminably long. Tim finally got his chance to say his piece for Universal to the few hundred people still in the room. He did well. He just "let the Holy Spirit guide him" as he called for Christian broadcasters to restrain themselves from any criticism or action against *The Last Temptation of Christ* until the "selected Christian leaders" had had a chance to attend the screening and give input to Universal on the anticipated response from Christian community. He assured them that Scorsese had promised to make a film that was an "affirmation of faith" and that Universal had committed that the Christian leaders would have a chance to see the film and give input on it "far in advance of the release date." The NRB delegates responded in anticipated good faith upon hearing these reassuring words from "one of their own."

Universal leadership must have had some doubts about

Tim, the statement he was to make, or the dynamics of the NRB, because they dispatched another paid representative to the NRB for purposes known only to them. Tim knew this guy was from another public relations firm and that he was assigned to the same Universal project. Tim and I wondered aloud if he was checking up on Tim, but dismissed the idea because we had nothing to hide. At times, though, it was a little funny, because this guy was philosophically and by lifestyle like a fish out of water with more than four thousand evangelical Christians. Furthermore, he "appeared" conveniently just about everywhere Tim and I went. He certainly was "present and accounted for" at the session at which Tim made his presentation.

When Tim got back in communication with the Universal bosses upon his return to California, they indicated in rather extravagant terms how pleased they were with his performance at NRB and with the statement he had made. When Tim inquired about the source of their information, they said that they had listened to the tape of the session! It was an insult to our integrity to think that Universal might have paid a high priced PR man thousands in fees and expenses to make sure Tim did his job. Regardless, U.P. apparently got good words from their "observer" at NRB.

Ignoring the whole matter, Tim got back to the task of lining up the attendees for the June screening. Billy Graham probably would not be able to attend. Tim got no response from Jerry Falwell's staff despite repeated attempts to reach him. Donald Wildmon of the American Family Association was preparing to send out millions of pieces of mail stirring up believers about "Universal's blasphemous film." He would hold off on the mailing if he was assured that this wasn't a trick.

He had "been burned before" and wasn't going to be burned again.

Dr. James Dobson of the Focus on the Family ministry could come to the screening. Dr. Lloyd John Ogilvie, senior minister at Hollywood Presbyterian Church planned to attend. Dr. Bill Bright, president of Campus Crusade for Christ could adjust his schedule to be there and seemed eager. He had been desiring to make contact with heads of major studios to open channels of communication with them. Dr. Jack Hayford of Church on the Way in Van Nuys would be able to make it. Tim suggested to Universal that it was vitally important that Archbishop Roger Mahoney be invited to attend, but Universal assured Tim that it was unnecessary.

As Tim approached these Christian leaders, he made sure that they felt completely comfortable about attending the screening. He always included the "worst case scenario" that Universal might put out a film that was destructive to Christ, and that, if it did, he wanted them to have made the decision without duress. He said frequently, "Don't listen to me. Listen to God and do what He tells you!" Tim planned to use the reponse of the leadership as a sort of "sign" that God was in the plan.

The days ticked off the calendar. Soon February was gone.

Tim and I talked often about the spiritual dynamics of his interaction with Pollock, Kornblitt, and Van Slyke --Tom, Si, and Sally--as the relationships deepened.

"I have told them over and over, Larry, that if they release a film that defames Jesus Christ, they will have to answer not only to the Christians but also to the God of Heaven and His Son."

"What do they say when you talk like that, Tim? Do they register any comprehension?"

"Well, they are very respectful. Tom and Si seem a little more uncomfortable with that kind of talk than Sally. They often respond with references to their Jewish heritage--implying to me that they are from a little different world."

"What about Sally?"

"Well, Sally and I have had some really good talks. She has an Episcopalian background and says that she believes in Christ. We have had some good talks about what constitutes a personal relationship with Christ. Her mother must be pretty religious; she warned Sally to stay away from *The Last Temptation* film."

I could tell that Tim liked all three of these people in different ways. From time to time we would pray for them and for God to use Tim in constructive ways in their lives. For now, it seemed that the way He wanted to do that was for Tim to do the very best he could in serving them in the consulting relationship. I was committed to helping Tim help them, and it was working.

Tim noticed that the cards and letters to Universal would taper off significantly after every major effort he made to get Christian leaders to hold their fire. Universal was giving Tim samples of letters that came in, many of which were lovely, sensitive appeals by all types of Christian believers asking the studio not to defame their Lord. Tim observed that it was these gracious, reasonable missives that seemed to make the most impact. As Tim's new working relationship developed, the press was generally unaware of the nature of it. The first disclosure in the press came in March in an article by Pat Broeske of the *Los Angeles Times*. "MCA/Universal is trying to defray worries [over *The Last Temptation of Christ*] by hiring a born again Christian marketing consultant who specializes in working with the Christian community." Ms. Broeske further described Tim's role as helping to "quell the talk until the film's available for screening." She quoted Tim as saying about the film, "Who can say what will happen? If you think what's happened with *Colors* is something, just wait." *Colors* was a film about street gangs which met with controversy because many in Los Angeles felt it would encourage more gang violence in a city already overrun with it.

Sally was obviously very, very uneasy about the article. Even though Universal publicity people had agreed to let Tim speak to Pat Broeske, they were not pleased with the content of the story. Sally warned that Tim "could expect 300 calls the next day from the press." Tom Pollock passed the word down to "remind Tim who he's working for." Tim didn't get a single call, and he kept his working priorities the same--God and Universal--in that order.

An awkward point in my relationship with Tim was the day that Universal told him they were getting letters from people who had been urged to write from a publication called *The Mediator*.

"Have you ever heard of *The Mediator*, Larry?" Tim asked.

"I am afraid I have, Tim." I replied. "That is the publication I put out to non-media people across America. Before we got involved in trying to build communication between Hollywood and the Christian community, I sent out an issue of *The Mediator* highlighting the situation with the film and urging people to write Universal. I haven't sent anything out since that one issue, and I am sorry if that has caused you difficulty. I promise you that I am not playing both ends against the middle."

"I trust you, Larry, and, as I tell all the Christian leaders with whom I speak about this, 'You have to do what you feel you must do to be obedient to God'."

"I know that, Tim, but so long as I am even indirectly tied to this effort with you and Universal, I will be loyal and supportive of what we are doing together to serve them and Hollywood's long term relationships with believers. You can be assured that when that time ends, I will sever my relationship with you to be free to obey my Lord."

"I know that, Larry. Every day I 'resign my position' with Universal to make sure I am serving Christ. I tell Him that if he does not want me in this relationship one more day, I'll resign. I'm not in this for the money, and I certainly am not about to sell out the Christian community for dollars!"

The passion with which Tim "resigned" each morning increased exponentially over the next few weeks. The more time that passed without any solid word about the content of the film and no opportunity to see it, the more certain members of the Christian community became restless. Donald Wildmon got more and more antsy as the days went by. He would call and ask if the screening was still on, as if he was seeking reassurance that it was. He kept saying things like, "Tim, this better not be a trick. I have never seen people respond as they are responding to this issue." Tim would assure him that, so far as he knew, the screening was still on, but I could tell that there was a growing uneasiness in Tim's mind.

Others would call asking if Universal leadership had shown any of the film to Tim. When he would answer that they hadn't, you could tell it was unsettling to him. "If you are their consultant, why won't they let you see it?" was a question he got often. He would endeavor to explain that the executives had not seen the film, that Scorsese hadn't finished putting it together, and that it was a "negative pickup" film, which means the production company doesn't see the film until the producer has it finished and is delivering it.

This was all the Universal "party line." At least one guy had a tough time believing it. It was the guy in the Key Man group who had numerous dealings with MCA. "Tim," he would say, "You've been in the film business long enough to know that you usually watch 'dailies' [the footage shot the previous day]. You can't tell me that if Lew Wasserman or Sid Sheinberg wanted to see some footage of this film there wouldn't be anything to see!"

I remember saying, "Tim, I can't imagine that Universal doesn't have *anything* to show you, so that you can represent them well. How can they expect you to speak with authority on their behalf if you don't even know with precision what is in the film? I think at some point you are going to have to demand to see what they have finished." Tim would agree and, in his gracious way, make another request to have access to the script, a rough cut, selected scenes, or something. He always got some answer that made it clear that to see the script or the film was either unlikely or impossible. At one point Sally indicated that she had seen the crucifixion scene, and that it was really moving. It brought her to tears. "Maybe Scorsese really is putting together a moving affirmation of faith," Tim suggested.

"Tim, any scene of a person being crucified is moving and ought to bring you to tears," I observed. "I think you have got to get a copy of the script or something. Your credibility is going to be zip after all of this time if Universal won't even let you have access to the content of the film you are trying to represent." Tim agreed and passed on another request.

Meanwhile, Tim was having an increasingly tough time just keeping his finger in the dike of Christian protest. The flood of letters pouring in to Universal was increasing daily now, and one of those letters was from Don Beehler, Dr. Bill Bright's director of communications for Campus Crusade for Christ. When a number of weeks had passed without a reponse, Don began wondering if Universal was answering its mail. Tim, learning of Beehler's situation, checked into it and found out that the executives really were not. When he checked specifically on Beehler's letter and found it unanswered, he warned the studio that it could not let important letters like that sit. He reminded them that Bill Bright represented a significant, worldwide ministry with the ability to influence great numbers of people in the global Christian community.

What followed was a hilarious "hot potato game" in which the execs first tussled over *what* was to be said, then over *how* it was to be said, then over *who* would *not* have to sign the letters! Tim recommended that they use a quote from an excellent article that had appeared in *Christianity Today* magazine as a result of an interview he had granted CT. Universal people had been very pleased with the article, so they agreed to excerpt the article in their letter. Tim wanted content from the CT article used because it was marked by openness and candor and because it committed Universal in writing to holding screenings for Christian leaders "far in advance" of the release date. The poor guy who ended up with the hot potato was not Wasserman, not Pollock, not Kornblitt, not Van Slyke. It was Roger Armstrong (hardly a household name at MCA) who is a Christian in the publicity department!

The letter which ended up in Don Beehler's mailbox, and in the mailboxes of many others who wrote the company in the early stages of the protest, read:

March 4, 1988

Dear Mr. Beehler,

We, at Universal Pictures, appreciate your letter of inquiry about "The Last Temptation of Christ."

We understand that there are many untrue rumors circulating about the movie. Since you have taken the time to write us, we would like to share with you the thoughts and desires of the director about his motion picture.

"'The Last Temptation of Christ' is a motion picture that I have wanted to make for over fifteen years. Both as a filmmaker and a Christian, I believe with all my heart that the film I am making is a deeply religious one. Although Jesus is tempted by Satan, what the movie says and what I believe is that Jesus resisted temptation and was crucified as told in the Bible. I have made a film which is an affirmation of faith and I urge everyone not to judge my film until they see it."

With great sincerity,
Martin Scorsese

As reported in the news section of the March 4, 1988, edition of *Christianity Today*, our Christian consultant, Tim Penland, in association with Universal Pictures, will hold advance screenings of the film for a select group of evangelical leaders far in advance of the release of the picture.

We appeal to your sense of fairness in this matter and it is our hope that you will delay judgment until you see the film.

Sincerely,

(Signed)

Roger Armstrong

If the objective was to build bridges between the Christian communty and Universal, this letter makes it sound as if that dream is fulfilled. Note the tone and wording of Scorsese's statement and his identification of himself as a "Christian." Note the commitment to hold the screenings for evangelicals "far in advance of the release of the picture." Note the appeal to "fairness."

The letter gave no position for Roger Armstrong, the poor guy who drew the "short straw" and had to sign the letter. Also, the execs must not have wanted to draw any more phone calls than they were getting, because the letterhead said, "Direct Dial Number," but the number had been whited out!

With word about the film getting around more rapidly now, there was an increasing number of ministers who weren't about to hold off *anything* when they saw an opportunity to get the jump on such a red hot issue. Some were beginning to mobilize without the benefit of hard knowledge about the film.

As the pressure mounted, Tim became more and more directive with the execs at Universal. Time and again he warned them of the consequences of taking believers too lightly. He remembers the day he stood in the offices of the Black Tower and told them, "You would be wise to deal with the Christian community with openness and candor or expect to look out this window some day and see 25,000 to 35,000 people protesting in front of your building." At that point none of us thought it would come to that.

I learned of one especially persistent group the day Tim said, "Larry, have you ever heard of The Evangelical Sisterhood of Mary?"

"Can't say as I have, Tim. Who are they?

"They describe themselves as an international movement of repentance. They are based in Germany and have their representatives in a number of countries. I think they are just a few hundred strong, but are they ever determined! I'm having difficulty getting them to hold off their response to this film until there is a screening. They keep saying things like, 'But this is an attack on our Lord. We can't stand by and let someone blaspheme our Savior!' And, frankly, I agree with them. I just tell them what I tell the other leaders, 'I can't tell you what to do but to be obedient to God. You will have to do whatever He directs. I am just asking you to consider holding off'."

"I'm not sure I would want to square off with a group of godly, praying women, Tim. Universal may be in for it with this bunch. Women with that kind of 'holy boldness' can be a mighty powerful force!"

"I agree, Larry. It will be interesting to see just what develops with this group. I will say this, those ladies have been more insistent and persistent to get to the bottom of this than anybody else."

In one of Tim's periodic reports to Universal about his "damage control" efforts, Tim mentioned the Evangelical Sisterhood of Mary and its persistence in pursuing the issue of this film and its contents. He was told, "We're not going to worry about a bunch of little old ladies."

Perhaps Tom, Si, and Sally could be excused for such a naive remark. From the standpoint of the leadership of a three and a half *billion* dollar corporate giant, who

40

would worry about a threat from a few hundred praying women?

They could be excused because they probably had never read the words of the Apostle Paul:

> God has deliberately chosen to use ideas
> the world considers foolish and of little worth
> in order to shame those people considered by
> the world as wise and great. He has chosen a
> plan despised by the world, counted as nothing
> at all, and used it to bring down to nothing
> those the world considers great, so that no
> one anywhere can ever brag in the presence of
> God.
>
> I Corinthians 1:27-29 LB

41

3

Crumbling Abutments

"They're going to let me see a script, Larry. Sally Van Slyke just called, and they are sending a script over now. As soon as I have a chance to look it over, I'll call you."

With these words Tim launched a new era of our involvement in the ongoing saga of the "mysterious film from Universal." I was as eager as Tim to take a look at this document because it would provide our first evidence of the content of the film. Even if it was a few months too late, the script finally would tell us what we had to do to keep our integrity. If this was a "faith affirming film," as Pollock and Scorsese had declared, it would be a relief and a joy to mobilize millions of American believers and non-believers alike to see "something good out of Hollywood." If this film was just a rehash of Kazantzakis' book with its hideous distortions of the person and work of Jesus, we would have our marching orders. Either way, it would be great to have some closure on the true nature of this project.

Time and again we asked ourselves, "What if this is a trap? What if Universal is leading us down the primrose path? What if Wasserman's troupe is leading us to slaughter?" And time and again we countered with, "If they are lying to us, that blood is on their hands. The Book tells us that Christ-like love " . . . always protects, always trusts, always hopes, always perseveres . . . ." (I Corinthians 13:7 NIV). Universal was responsible for itself. We weren't responsible!

Even before we got the script, we were getting information about those involved with the project that should have prepared us better than it did for its contents. First, Scorsese was clearly a highly unlikely candidate to create anything approaching the "inspirational" or "faith affirming." When his name came up in a Key Man meeting right at the outset, one producer with hundreds of hours of prime time TV and a number of motion pictures to his credit said, "Scorsese? A film on Christ from Scorsese? You're in trouble. Scorsese is a dark director." I didn't know what that meant, but I listened intently as these professionals discussed the style and technique of one of their peers. The producer went on to describe *Taxi Driver* and *Raging Bull*. "Martin isn't capable of producing anything with goodness and light. He's preoccupied with the sinister side, the dark side, the occult side of life and of characters!"

If a man's creative work is the result of his experiences, we might have been able to predict some of Scorsese's film content. A man who has experienced the trauma of three previous marriage failures might be expected to project a somewhat low view of women in his work. A man who has been kicked out school while studying for the Catholic priesthood might be expected to create a "put down" of certain symbols and sacraments held dear by Catholics, if not a put down of Jesus. But not knowing much about Scorsese, these bases for prediction failed us.

The same could be said for Paul Schrader, the writer of the screenplay. Had we known more about Schrader, about his rearing in a Christian home, his graduation from Calvin College--a protestant, Christian Reformed denominational school--and his antipathy to his former faith, it would have helped. If we had known then that Schrader views Christ as "an existential pacifist," a "tormented soul," and a "wimpy beatnik," we might have been better able to predict the product that would be in our hands when the script from Universal arrived.[9] But, once again, we were blindsided. Schrader was hardly a household word in Hollywood writing circles despite his collaboration with Scorsese in *Taxi Driver, Raging Bull, American Gigolo,* and other projects.

We should have processed all of this data more thoroughly than we did. We would have been in a better position to evaluate the script when it came.

I guess I really should say "a" script, not "the" script, because the call from Sally created an aura of mystery around the script we were sent that was not unlike the mystery we felt surrounding the film. When Sally said, "We're sending over a script," Tim asked, "Is this *the* script?" "I don't know, Tim, whether it is the final one or what." Sally seemed secretive, hesitant. She said the script came from a department with a name we didn't recognize, the "continuity department" or something. She didn't ask for comments, seemed quite uneasy, and didn't want to talk about it. Tim dismissed much of this for the time being. The "mysterious" script arrived, and he began to pour over it. I awaited his call with considerable eagerness. The call finally came.

"Larry, we have some *big* problems! I have just read through this script, and I don't see any way it can be salvaged. If this is a faith affirming film, I don't know whose faith! Let me read you some passages." Tim read the scene where Jesus is sitting with other customers of prostitute Mary Magdalene in the entrance to her brothel where Magdalene is having sex. He read the tongue kissing scene between John the Baptist and Jesus to which Jesus responds, "His tongue felt like a burning coal in my mouth." He read me Mary's statement about her son, "Forgive my son! He's crazy! He doesn't know what he's doing. He has problems. Ever since he was a baby. He's not well in the head." He read me Jesus' sex scene with Magdalene in the dream sequence: "Jesus and Magdalene make love on blankets spread over the straw. He kisses her breasts, her lips."

That was a long call. Tim explained that he had marked potentially offensive content on 80 of the 120 pages of the script!

"What do you think I should do now, Larry?" Tim asked.

"I don't think you have any alternative but to indicate your concerns to Universal. You need to tell them that screening is going to be a real dandy if the Christian leaders who are invited are asked to sit through this stuff! If they don't believe you, the Christian leaders certainly will convince 'em!"

"That will probably end my relationship with Universal."

"Maybe so, but you have been 'resigning' every day anyhow, haven't you?"

"I sure have."

"Well, Tim, maybe this is the day when your resignation gets accepted!"

We had a good laugh, the kind of laugh we often had in discussing these heavy matters. We frequently played a kind of Oliver and Hardy role with each other in which one would say to the other, "Now look at the fine mess you've got me in!"

Universal seemed extremely edgy about loaning the script to Tim. The *very next day* Tim got a terse call from Sally's secretary at Universal indicating that "all scripts were being called in" and that a courier was on his way over to Tim's office in Burbank to retrieve it! The secretary seemed ruffled, as if to say without saying it, "You have no business having a script" or "we never should have let you have one" or something akin to that. Tim had had the script barely twenty-four hours! Since I had not even had a chance to see the actual document, I explored the possibility of his making a copy. Tim was adamant that, while he was not specifically prohibited from making a copy, he did not feel that any copies should be made. As if he had some premonition that it might return to haunt him, he felt deeply that he didn't even *want* a copy in his possession. End of discussion.

If Tim had had difficulty defending his position with Universal to Christian leaders *before* seeing the script, it was becoming more difficult by the day! For weeks we discussed daily whether "this was the day" to execute a resignation. Tim held off thinking (1) that he might be able to influence the final form of the film, (2) that he might convince Universal not to release it, (3) that even though the script was certainly horrific, there was a strong possibility the finished film would

46

be quite different, and (4) that he was in a weak position to make a final judgment not having seen the film. "How can we wisely make a decision on a film we haven't seen?" was a question we asked ourselves. We were going to hear *that* question again. He also kept remembering how strongly Scorsese had stated that the final film would be "faith affirming."

The most important reason Tim stayed on, though, was that he hadn't heard God's direction to leave, even though he was listening intently. We kept thinking that if we could only hold out until the screening, the Christian leaders would reinforce our position and convince the studio that this film was going to be a real disaster in the Christian community. We began to plan lifeboat strategies and sketch worst case scenarios.

"Tim," I suggested, "the most crucial element of this affair is the span of time between the screening and the release date of the film. If Universal is using us to hold off protests so they can profit from the controversy, and if they do release a film over the protests of the Christian community, the Christian leaders need some time to mobilize protests."

"That is what Wildmon keeps saying," Tim responded, "that he isn't going to let Universal push him into a position in which he has no response time after the screening. That's why he has said mid-June is the non-negotiable limit. He needs three months' lead time to sound the alarm to his constituency. He's saying he's prepared to put a million dollars into fighting Universal if they do a number on him."

"He'll do it, too. He's a real street fighter. But the other Christian leaders will need response time too!

We have to do what we can to protect them or our names really will be mud! If that happens, I am going to tell people all of this was *your* idea. 'Tim Penland?' I'll say, 'Never heard of the guy!'"

Tim knew I was kidding. We both agreed that the lack of knowledge of the true contents of the film made our job more difficult, but we still were banking on the screening to be the turning point in the whole affair.

As it turned out, the screening *wasn't* the turning point. The *script* was! I don't mean the mysterious script from Universal, I mean *another* script! Donald Wildmon had intimated to us earlier that he thought he could get a script. He wasn't saying how or where, he was just saying he thought he could get one. Tim and I didn't put much stock in that until the day Tim got a call from Tupelo, Mississippi, Wildmon's headquarters.

"Hey, Tim, I got a script, and this movie is terrible! I am having two hundred copies duplicated right now. I'll drop a copy in the mail to you. I'm thinking of sending them out to the heads of church denominations, and I'm going to do it right away unless Universal delays the release of the film." Universal obviously wasn't going to delay the release, so Wildmon sent them out.

When the script arrived, we poured over it. It was, for all intents and purposes, very much the same script as Tim had seen. The one Universal had sent over was 120 pages, this one was 99. That could have been due largely to retyping. This one had no copyright protection on it. It did have notes in the margins in which someone had marked scenes that were and were not in Kazantzakis' book. Page numbers in the margins

48

referenced the sections of the book that were in the screenplay, and a crude, hand drawn cross was on the title page above *The Last Temptation of Christ*.

This script spread across the country like a firestorm. Everybody who got a copy must have made at least a dozen copies and distributed them. Some heads of denominations sent copies to every one of their ministers! In a few weeks my office had made hundreds, most of which went to Christian professionals in film and television and to heads of Christian ministries. In just a few days phone lines were buzzing all across the continent about the contents of the script and the need to stop this horrible attack on Christ from being released.

Tim told Universal that Wildmon was distributing a copy of the script. We assumed, though we had no evidence to support it, that some employee at Universal had spirited the script out of the walls of the Black Tower. Tim suggested that Universal probably would want to check out its security for future reference! On this one, it was too late.

"Tim," I told my buddy, "It's obvious to me that your days are numbered at Universal! Now that this script is out, it makes no difference about screenings, what's in the film, what you say, what Christian leaders say, or what Universal says. Pollock and company are now accountable for what is in the circulated script. Sure, there are some differences between the script you saw and this one, but they are not substantial enough to worry about. *This script* is now the issue!"

"I agree, Larry. But with such a short time 'til the screening, do you think I ought to hang in there and follow through with that?"

"Whatever you think God wants you to do, Tim. But I think that every day the Christian community knows the contents of that script and knows you are continuing to represent Universal, you appear to be a traitor to the cause. Even if you were disposed to staying on, you can't really serve Universal any more. This thing is out of your hands. *God has taken it* out of your hands!"

We prayed for God's wisdom as we often did on our phone calls. Then we discussed a course of action. We decided that Tim would make one last check with the Universal trio to confirm that the screening date was still on and to make one last request to see the film.

Even before Tim's final request, we had begun to sense that something was seriously awry at Universal. Tim had been having a real deuce of a time getting calls back from the executive suite, Universal had been running behind in its payments to him, and he had sensed some "waffling" when the subject of the screening came up. I had encouraged him to pursue it and to nail them on the screening date, if nothing else.

Tim followed through. I couldn't believe my ears when Tim reported back on the second of June.

"Well, Larry, I had my meeting. Met with Sally at 11:30 this morning. She says that they are getting phone calls like crazy!"

"What did she say about the screening?"

"Bad news. She says that they can't hold a screening any earlier than the third week in July, maybe even in

August."

"What? You're kidding!"

"No, I am not kidding!"

"Why not?

"They say that Scorsese doesn't have the film ready, and they don't know when he will."

"Tim, that's nonsense! There is no way they can be heading for an early October release of the film and have 'no idea' when it can be seen! What about the letters of invitation that went to the Christian leaders for June 10?"

"We didn't talk about that, but I told them that there was no way that I could continue under these conditions. Si came in and suggested that I not leave now. He thought by the middle of next week 'maybe' he could get me a 'rough' date in July!"

"Well, then, are they going to move up the release date accordingly?"

"I asked them that. They said they couldn't do *that!* They have release schedules to honor!"

"Tim, we have been ripped off! They are just trying to rob the Christians of time to respond and are trying to play off the rising controversy!"

"It sure looks like that, doesn't it. I think I have to resign now for sure."

"Tim, I agree. *Yesterday* would have been a better day! If I were you, I would give them a conditional resignation letter. If they don't meet the conditions, the resignation takes effect automatically."

Tim started to write a memo to Universal. He struggled with it. He tried to tell them *again* that they had *big* problems. He couldn't get the letter to flow. He worked on it, left it, and came back to it a number of times. The memo sat unfinished for five hours. Finally, he gave up, went home, and retired for the evening.

At 2:00 a.m. he was awakened as if by some cosmic alarm clock. As he lay there struggling in his mind over the memo, he got the answer: "Tim, the memo won't flow until you put your resignation in it!" That was it! God was telling him the time was *now!* He accepted the decision he knew was God's and went back to sleep. When Tim returned to what was now unmistakably a "resignation memo" the next morning, June 3, he finished it in minutes. He took it over to Universal immediately. The effective date of the resignation was June 12 if Universal did not meet his conditions.

The clock now ticking on Tim's resignation memo, it seemed that events were "piling up," converging on us in time and space to make the decision regarding our relationship with Universal more and more clear. One of these events was the appearance of a tiny, June 4 article in the *Philadelphia Inquirer* saying:

> Martin Scorsese clearly anticipates trouble when he releases his newest film, *The Last Temptation of Christ* in the fall. In the spring, he signed on a Christian marketing expert to

shepherd the movie past possible objections of religionists. Now comes word that he has scheduled a series of secret New York screenings . . . .

Tim was livid! If this quote was accurate, it seemed apparent that Universal had been *playing him for a sucker all along and had been using him to betray his own brethren for its benefit!*

Tim sought immediate counsel from a trusted, top executive with another major studio regarding these developments. The exec said, "Tim, they have just kicked this project up to the top guy. Quit talking to the people at the second level. Get on the phone immediately with Tom Pollock and confront him with this article. Demand to see that film immediately! If he hesitates a split second, run as fast as you can! They *have* the completed film. There is absolutely no reason they wouldn't show it to you, *unless* they are using you and know they can't continue to use you once you've seen it."

Tim hung up the phone and dialed Tom Pollock's office as fast as he could push the buttons. Surprisingly, Si Kornblitt answered and sought to handle Tim. "Si, I can't explain to you what I need to discuss. I've got to talk to Tom Pollock!" Si nervously put Tom on the line.

Tim began, "Tom, I am looking at an article from the *Philadelphia Inquirer* that is going to have me mowing lawns next week, if I'm lucky."

"What do you mean, Tim?"

Tim read him the parts that said he had been hired to

"shepherd the film past possible objections of religionists," and that indicated Scorsese was scheduling secret screenings. The interchange between Tom and Tim is reconstructed as closely as we can here.

Pollock said, "Tim, I don't know anything about this."

"Tom, this story is painting me as a hired gun for Universal. I find it very offensive personally and defaming to the very respected leaders that I have brought into this. I must go immediately to the press and explain to them that I have been used."

"Now wait a minute, Tim," Tom replied, almost frantically, "If you quit now, you will kill this film."

"Why would you say that?"

"Tim, anything you have to say to the press about this film right now will be viewed as very negative. You don't understand what we have here. This film will be a great work of art, even if it is somewhat controversial." Tom was talking fast and selling for all he was worth. "I tell you what we'll do. You, Scorsese, and I will go before the press and denounce this news story as false."

"It's too late, Tom. With this in circulation, my job is over! I find it very offensive that Martin Scorsese would be so blatantly candid to the press as to what *he* perceives my role to be. He must have gotten that idea from someone else. He surely didn't get it from me! Tom, you have to have seen the film. *Why won't you let me see it?*"

"Tim," Tom replied, stammering a bit as he is known to

do when he's under pressure, "the film is on a bunch of reels, and it's just impossible for you to see it right now."

"Tom, with that script circulating and you refusing to let me see this film, there is no way I can help you any longer. I can promise you that the Christian leaders who have seen that script will *make you eat that script paaage by paaage!*"

Tom continued to try to get Tim to cooperate in a press appearance, but Tim wasn't buying it. After some more interaction, Tim half-heartedly agreed to work on a press release denouncing the *Enquirer* story, a release which Si and the others frantically wrote and rewrote that afternoon. Despite the frenzied preparation, that statement apparently was never released to the press at large. It surfaced only at a few *Christian* periodicals!

It was all over. On June 12 the dream of building a bridge between the Christian community and Hollywood collapsed. Tim's resignation became effective. On June 14, Tim's journal entry read, "Met with Sally and Si and worked out final wording of [resignation] news release and parted company 'friendly' ?!?"

Despite Tim's departure, Universal still tried desperately to convince the "core group" of Christian leaders whom Tim had secured that the studio would, indeed, hold a screening for them . . . on July 12. After the duplicity they had experienced with Pollock and company, the Christian leaders would not cooperate. They were not going to allow themselves to be exploited further and would not attend a screening that their representative, Tim Penland, did not host. This gave rise to the oft-quoted half-truth, "Christian leaders protesting the film were invited to a screening by Universal which they refused to attend."

The bridge abutments had been crumbling for weeks, but now all of the Christian community's effort, good faith, hope, and trust that had been laid block upon block in that bridge collapsed.

In a variation of this metaphor, Tim told a reporter, "Just when I thought the bridge was about complete, I saw a Mack truck coming over it right at me!" For my money Tim misread the make. That was an *MCA truck,* an eighteen wheeler bearing mud flaps with chrome plated nudes, dollar signs for grillwork, and "What a friend we have in Jesus" on the trailer. It's no fun being run over by a three and half billion dollar truck. It's less fun being run over by drivers in whom you've placed your trust.

It does seem to be poetic justice, however, that the script that turned the Christian world on its ear fell into the hands of those "little old ladies" whom Universal had ridiculed, those *praying* ladies of the Evangelical Sisterhood of Mary who proved themselves to be neither "little" enough nor "old" enough to take lightly. Those in the MCA driver's seat should have heeded the ladies' notice that read, "DANGER. SEVERE TIRE DAMAGE!"

4

Shots Are Fired

Now that Tim was an "alumnus" of Universal Pictures, we both were flooded with a great sense of relief. That working relationship was a little like sliding down a bannister and watching it turn into a razor blade. We both were happy to be off the bannister!

Taking one final look back at his departure from the folks in the Black Tower, Tim shared with me one poignant memory. After a final encounter with the Universal triumvirate, Sally Van Slyke had said almost admiringly to the others, "There goes a man who did nothing but try to help us." When Tim related that to me in his own uncomplicated manner, I felt a warm sense of the rightness of what we had done for them. I couldn't help thinking that, in some ultimate metaphysical dimension, that is what life should be all about, *doing nothing but trying to help.* I felt fortunate to be Tim's friend and comrade in arms.

If there ever was any doubt about our commitments, it seemed clear that now really was the time to be comrades in arms. How many times I had heard Tim say, "Larry, I told them *again* that if they release a film defaming my Lord, that will be the end of my relationship with them. I'll be out there on the picket lines!" The fact that there weren't any picket lines to join didn't deter us. We did what we had done every other time we were up against it. We prayed.

I am sure this whole "prayer business" is a mystery to

most of our peers in film and TV. The Lichter and Rothman research on the values of media's elite indicated that 93% of media leadership seldom or never attend a religious ceremony of any kind.[10] Very few (13%) ever read any sacred scriptures and only a minority (40%) ever pray. Prayer surely was not a common practice for the Universal troupe, and it generally isn't in Hollywood.

I'll never forget the time I was meeting with a top executive in the industry and, after a brief and cordial chat, prepared to leave. As I exited from this first visit, I asked if I would offend him if I prayed for him. Somewhat surprised, he consented. So I grabbed his hand and uttered a short but earnest prayer. I looked up to see moisture in his eyes as I left. He later told me that in all the years he had been in the film and TV business nobody had ever prayed for him in his office.

By now Tim and I had become ardent "pray-ers." Working with Universal surely enriched our prayer lives! We prayed about what we were to do, and we prayed about how we were to do it. We prayed about what we were supposed to say, and we prayed about how we were to say it. On most of the hundreds of phone calls linking Tim's office and mine or Tim's home and mine, we would pray about our current situation, for each other, for the folks at Universal. We certainly weren't going to enter a scary new phase of the escalating tensions with the *Last Tempation* gang without seeking and finding God's direction. We had committed early in our relationship that we wouldn't pursue a course of action unless we felt *as one man* that it was what God wanted us to do. We figured that if we both were being led by the Spirit of God, we would be unified.

58

We also checked everything at the level of our human spirits. Even though Tim graciously told me when we entered this covenant that he was going to look to me for confirmation of God's guidance, it never was one way guidance. Repeatedly one of us could be heard saying to the other, "I just don't feel right about that in my spirit" or "I have real peace in my spirit about that course of action." In a world where the spiritual dimension of life is ridiculed as unscientific or mixed with hocus pocus as in ouija boards and horoscopes, seeking spiritual guidance from the Spirit of God must sound a little bizarre. But Tim and I believe with all our hearts the statement made in the New Testament by the Apostle Paul, "Those who are led by the Spirit of God are the sons of God . . . . The Spirit himself testifies with our spirit that we are God's children" (Romans 8:14,16 NIV). Nearly every time we sought God's direction some new development broke into the open. This time, within a few days of Tim's resignation, was no exception.

"Larry!" Tim's voice sounded urgent. "You'll never guess what I just found out! If God hasn't answered our prayers!"

"What is it, Tim?"

"I just got a call from a person close to one of the top people at Universal. It now appears certain that they have been lying to us. Universal screened the film for their distribution people and the film is even worse than the script!"

"What? You mean they had it ready to screen for their distribution people, but they didn't have it to show to you or the Christian leaders?"

59

"That's what I mean. This insider who saw the film said it is so terrible that he has refused to be associated with it. He knows his decision isn't going to be popular, but he is enough of a Christian that he is willing to take the risk. He hasn't been able to sleep nights, he is so troubled about the picture. The guy I talked to is a very committed Christian who has been agonizing with him. He felt, after praying a lot about it, that he had to call me and let me know this."

"That was a pretty gutsy thing to do. It would be great if he could give us a little better picture of the specific contents of the film."

"It surely would, Larry, but I know the guy fears for his job. He has been with Universal a number of years."

"Oh, that's just what Universal needs in the middle of this--a 'wrongful dismissal' suit for firing a guy for his religious beliefs!"

"I hope it won't come to that. I have no permission to reveal the name of the man, the name of his close confidant, or his position inside the structure. We'll just have to see if we can at least get precise information about the content of the film and the treatment of the script."

During the next few weeks, in late June and early July, this high level informant was able to clarify key points in the content of the film. This was invaluable to us. Since we had seen a script, there were few surprises about the basic content of the film, but there were a *lot* of surprises as to how certain scenes were shot.

This man, whom we dubbed "The Unnamed Source," described the explicit nature of the sex scene between Jesus and Magdalene, the scene in which the disciples are taking the bread and cup at the last supper only to have the wine turn into blood in their mouths and come dripping out, the full, female, frontal nudity at the baptism of Jesus, and other treatments not perceptible from reading the script. He informed us that the print he saw was 2 hours and 48 minutes long, information that revealed that Scorsese's later editing to clean up some of the more offensive content--including the sex scene--took eight minutes out of the picture.

We later got word that Universal executives joked around the Black Tower about one person they thought must be The Unnamed Source: "Has The Unnamed Source arrived for the meeting yet, George?" "No, The Unnamed Source called in saying he would be a little late today."

The most revealing information coming from The Unnamed Source was not the visual treatments given the script by Scorsese, but the fact that *within seven days* of the scheduled screening for Christian leaders --for which the film "wasn't ready"--it was ready enough to show to Universal distribution people! This is the same film Tim was told couldn't be seen until late July or early August!

This was the final nail in the coffin of any presumed good faith on the part of the Black Tower in dealing with Christians. It now appeared to us as if when the trinity at the top of Universal was patting Christians on the back, they were merely doing so to find a soft spot to stab them.

It was time to mobilize for war.

As Tim and I talked strategy, we determined that we had to act fast, and we had to get the word of Universal's planned release of this monster out to as many Christians across America as rapidly as possible. We had to act fast because it seemed as if Universal was, as the Government would say it, "dealing in disinformation" with its revised release date of September 23. More than one source inside Universal and inside the industry tipped us off that they were gunning for an early release to capture the peak of the controversial free publicity. The mid-June screening for their own distribution people also supported this. They were operating "full spead ahead" and we knew it!

We also knew we had to get to as many Christians as possible because, otherwise, there was no way we could see a sufficient response generated to catch Universal's attention before the release. We didn't have any trouble finding angry Christian leaders with whom to start. There already were a good number of heads of ministries, those who had been invited to the "nonexistent screening" and who were infuriated at being exploited by a major American corporation in which they had placed their trust. They were ready to singe the ears of their constituencies with the account of Universal's rejection of their good faith attempts to serve Hollywood's movie giant.

While interacting with Don Beehler, Bill Bright's communication director, Tim and the others came up with the idea of a conference call among the offended brethren. It was decided that the call could take place on Saturday, June 25th. Bright, Dobson, Wildmon, Hayford, Ogilvie, and Penland were on the line.

The call was a sharing of anger over the incredible insult that had been dealt to them, a mapping of strategy for dealing with the situation, and an agreement that each of them would send communication to Universal immediately expressing his offense. Each would indicate that he would not attend any future screening and would demand that his personal name not be used in any way in association with the film. The men agreed to keep in touch as the strategy developed further.

I knew that we had to get to the Christian community --and fast. I whipped out a letter to the Mastermedia constituency relaying the taunt that came from inside Universal, "The Christians aren't going to stop us from releasing this film." I attributed the quote to Tom Pollock, and referred to this arrogant attack on the Christian community as "the moral equivalent of Pearl Harbor." My staff team hustled to get the epistle into the hands of the few thousand who receive our letter.

I knew Donald Wildmon was running hard to get his million or more mailing out, but I also knew his system had a "turn around" time of more than two months! In two months the film could be in distribution! We had to find a way to get to more people faster! Tim and I racked our brains.

"Tim, I think our best bet is James Dobson's radio program, *Focus on the Family*. Dr. Dobson has a broader following among Christians than most Christian broadcasters, has incredible respect and credibility, and has the most widely syndicated program in radio, either secular or religious. I know his program is aired on more than a thousand stations. Jim's a wonderful friend, and, if he would let us go on his program with our story, I know we would see phenomenal, immediate response!"

"Sounds like a great idea. I certainly would be willing to go on the program, if you could set it up. I know Dr. Dobson is angry at the way he and the others have been handled. He just might agree to it. How fast can he get the program to air?"

"That may be a problem. He has a "turn around" time of more than a month, but I also know that he sometimes preempts his programming to deal with time sensitive issues. I think we must have until at least August before Universal can get the thing to the theaters, don't you think?"

"I would think so, but I have known of production companies getting a film to the theaters in less than 30 days from the point of the finished master."

"We'll just have to trust the Lord for His timing and go for it!"

We went for it! Dr. Dobson graciously consented to have us on his program, and we scheduled the taping for June 30. The afternoon of the taping Tim and I met for lunch to go over the flow of content we wanted to share. I had briefed Dobson's production people so that they could brief Dobson. After lunch, a brief "talk through" of the content and prayer, Tim and I headed over to the studios.

It had been a terrible week for Dr. Dobson. His mother had died only a few days previously, he was overwhelmed with obligations backed up from his personal crisis, he was to leave for an African trip in a

64

few days, and the Focus on the Family headquarters was in a frenzy. About an hour off schedule, we met briefly in Dr. Dobson's office before hitting the studio. He confessed that, with all that was going on in his life, he had not had a chance to look over the briefing material on the program. After sketching briefly the anticipated flow of the interview, Tim spoke.

"Dr. Dobson, I think I need to say that I may not be able to come out very strongly on this program. I am still weighing my future in the film business and think that it might be better for Dr. Poland, here, to take the lead in calling the Christians to action."

There was a pregnant pause before Jim said, "Now look, Tim, if Larry and I are coming across an 8 on a scale of 10 in emotion and you are coming across a 2, you are going to make us both look silly. You better decide right now what it is going to be."

"Okay, Dr. Dobson. I see your point. I am going to take that as the voice of the Lord to me. You can count on me to be with you men."

That was a major cutting of the emotional apron strings for Tim. Any ties to Universal, to his future in the film business, to any personal fears or reluctance to commit fully to this cause were fatally injured with that challenge from Dobson. From that *minute* on Tim was sworn into the army for this war. He had passed the point of no return.

The show went well. All three of us were at least an 8, probably closer to a 9, in emotional charging. We laid out the contents of the film, the history of our working relationship with Universal, and the announced determination of Universal to release the movie. We called Christians to a telephone and letter writing effort to get the studio to stop the release. Focus on the Family offered a "Fact Sheet" for listeners built partly on the one I had prepared for the Mastermedia list.

In the middle of the program I had mentioned that this film could hit the theaters in as little as thirty days. Dobson stopped the taping and addressed his crew.

"When is the program scheduled to air?"

"If we preempt some other content, probably in about four weeks, sir."

"Any way we can get it there sooner? If Universal scrambles, that may give our listeners only a few days of response time. I don't want to miss this one!"

The staff conferred a bit and then suggested, "If we really push it and double it up with the special program you are going to do about the passing of your mother, we should be able to get it to air in two weeks, by Monday, July 11."

"Great, let's do it!" was Dr. Dobson's reply. The taping continued.

My heart leaped in my chest. That was the day before a screening that Universal was scheduling for "religious leaders" in New York City. It seemed like perfect timing! Tim and I were exultant. The first missile was fired, and it would hit on July 11!

When I got back to my office, my staff people had been doing some thinking on their own. We had talked briefly before about creating some vehicle for the hundreds of Christians in film and television to express themselves about this film. We felt it would be a good watershed point for some of them who had been "secret agents" or "woodwork Christians" in Hollywood for years. If they came out identifying themselves as Christians in Tinseltown, there would be no turning back. It could make a statement to the media community and would indicate that opposition to *The Last Temptation* was not just from the "religious right in Omaha."

I had conceived the idea as a full page ad statement in one of the trade magazines, signed, "Christian professionals in film and television" or something. I pounded out the copy:

CRUCIFY HIM! CRUCIFY HIM!

Two thousand years ago people who despised His person and rejected His message demanded that Jesus of Nazareth be condemned to death, despite the fact that His judge found no fault in Him. In the two millennia since His resurrection, hundreds of millions have found forgiveness, joy, power, and hope through faith in Him.

Today Universal Pictures is planning to release a Martin Scorsese film based on the Kazantzakis novel, *The Last Temptation of Christ*. This film maligns the character, blasphemes the deity, and distorts the message of Jesus.

**As professional members of the film and
television community, we demand that this
film not be released.**

**Whether the gain is a hundred million
dollars or thirty pieces of silver makes no
difference. Our Lord was crucifed once
on a cross. He doesn't deserve to be
crucifed a second time
on celluloid.**

I called Tim and read the copy to him. He seemed to like it.

"How are you going to have it signed, Larry?"

"Oh, I thought something like, 'Christian professionals in film and television'."

"You're not going to have people sign their names to the ad?"

"Well, I hadn't thought so."

"Poland, that is the wimpiest kind of statement I've ever heard." I had never heard Tim come across so strong. "If you don't have any names on the ad, it means nothing. I have been reading the trade papers for years, and when people make some statement like this, they always include names! Even if nobody reads the copy, *everybody* will read every single name!"

"I agree with you in principle, Tim. I just don't know how I can meet the deadline. I have to have the copy to *The Hollywood Reporter* by tomorrow. We have reserved a full page on the inside front cover. I don't know how I could get the copy to enough media Christians to get a response by the deadline."

"Don't you dare put that ad in without names." Tim was *booming* now! "Take this as a word from the Lord, Larry. Don't do it!"

I agreed inside that Tim was right. It had to have names. I put the Mastermedia staff on "red alert." We got *The Reporter* to give us a break on the deadline. We mailed packages with the challenge to join the effort, the proposed copy, and a response form for immediate return to 375 media professionals on our list. We made special efforts to get the packet to the Key Men, thinking they could help us get names on a personal level.

Everything went wrong. A spot check of people in L. A. indicated that few of them had gotten the packet the next day! When they did get it, some of them didn't think the ad was a good idea. Some wanted changes in the copy. Some thought the timing was bad. Some thought the copy had too much horseradish. Some obviously were frightened of the personal consequences of identifying openly as a Christian in the industry. *All* knew that it was a significant decision to be so openly indentified with Christ and an appeal to Universal not to release the film.

With twenty four hours to the deadline, we had fifteen or so names. We had promised the respondents that their names would not appear in an ad with fewer than thirty names. It looked like this idea was a disaster. Nothing like blowing your missile launcher apart on the second shot of the war!

My heart sank as my staff guy told me we had only a handful of names and just twenty-four hours to go. It surely didn't appear possible. When I faced a similar "impossible" situation years ago a dear, retirement aged missionary walked up to me and handed me a little 3 by 5 card on which was printed, "Difficulty is the environment for miracle; but if it is to be a very great miracle, the environment is not difficulty but impossibility." I remember praying, "Lord, if you want this to go, you'll have to make it work. If you don't, no problem. I just want what you want." I felt better having gotten the responsibility for this apparent failure off my chest.

The staff team scheduled a meeting at my computer for three o'clock the next afternoon. They would give me the names, I would crank them out on my laser printer, and we would get the copy to Federal Express by five o'clock. By the next morning we had twenty-one or twenty-two names after all of the mail was processed. Hopeless.

I got a call just after lunch indicating that the staff guy was on his way over with the list of names to enter.

"Do we have thirty names?" I asked tentatively.

"No, we have sixty-one!"

"Sixty-one? Where did they all come from?

"We got a bunch from CBS Television City including a vice president and other key people. Larry, I think this thing is going to catch on. I know of a number of other people who are collecting names, and we know of still others who have called to say they're sending in their names!"

"Incredible! Compared to twenty-four hours ago, this surely smells like a miracle, doesn't it?"

Up to the last minute I was still getting "input" on the ad from various quarters. With so many advertising, media, film, TV, PR, and marketing people responding, I was getting four opinions for every three people. Part of the insistence was due to the fact that this was going to bear *their names!* Some were adamant that we shouldn't put names in unless they were *big names*. They were *sure* we could get big names. For that matter, *I* was sure we could get big names. But that wasn't the point. These names were to represent sensitive, respected human beings, not celebrities. I knew, too, if we were to play the celebrity game, Universal could call in its chips and whip us 50 to 1! Who were we trying to kid?

All of the input did lead us to make some changes in the ad. Tim suggested we change the headline copy to read, "I find no fault in Him" with attribution to Pontius Pilate rather than "Crucify Him! Crucify Him!" Others agreed. Some felt it created a warmer tone for the ad. Others thought our Jewish friends in the industry might hear something we weren't saying if we used the "Crucify" language. Still others felt "demand" was too strong a word. I agreed. "Ask" was more in keeping with the reasoned approach we wanted to take.

Despite the numbers of people who read the ad before it went to press, nobody caught the fact that "deity" was misspelled "diety!" Later, as the controversy grew, we took it on the chin in the letters to the editor for "trying to defend something we didn't even know how to spell." We had a few good laughs at ourselves. Considering the rush to get the thing together and the pressure we were under, it's a wonder we spelled "Jesus" right! Just another of God's little ways of keeping us humble, we rationalized.

At the final hour, after the copy for the ad was already in the hands of the *Reporter*, one of my most trusted friends, a consummate professional in an executive position with one of the TV stations in town, called adamant that the timing on the ad was all wrong. He was willing to help raise the money to pay the *Reporter* for the ad which he wanted me to cancel. I responded, "I hear you. I respect you, and I can't defend my position logically. I just have this 'gut feeling' that this ad has to run on Monday. I hope it won't threaten our relationship if I make a decision different from the one you are recommending." He assured me it wouldn't, and I stuck to that confirmation in my spirit that the decision was absolutely right.

As it turned out, it was! Shot number two was on its way to the target and would also hit on July 11. Now for shot number three!

5

Preemptive Strike

As a freshman in college I was required to attend four classes in ROTC, Reserve Officer Training Corps, labeled by the college catalog as "Military Science and Tactics 101 - 104." The courses were losers unless you were bent on making a career of fighting wars.

The hours of classes I sat through over a two year span distilled out to precious little benefit *except* for some excellent lessons in dealing with authority, shinier shoes, and a page and a half of life-changing content in the military history class. In that class we studied battle strategies of great military conflicts over the ages which were reduced on a page and a half as the nine *universal* [no pun intended] principles of war. These were reputed to be the principles that have guided military men in warfare for centuries and are foundational to every military victory. I would have difficulty reciting all nine nearly thirty years later, but two that I remember clearly suited this situation with MCA/Universal nicely: "surprise" and "mass."

In the principle of "surprise" you try to keep your enemy off balance by continually operating at places and in ways that he least expects. In the principle of "mass" you endeavor to amass your firepower at the enemy's weakest point in order to achieve a decisive victory. While Tim and I went through no conscious listing of the "nine principles of war," we can see in retrospect that following the leading God gave us fleshed out most of those principles in genius fashion.

Certainly that was true of "shot number three" which hit the Black Tower on July 12--a press conference.

I mentioned earlier that Universal had planned a screening of *The Last Temptation* for a "select group" of religious leaders on July 12 in New York. This was, according to their party line, the "postponed" screening which the previously invited Christian leaders "refused to attend"--the clever but misleading half-truth I have referred to before. Universal needed some supportive comments by religious leaders regarding the film to help defend against the clerics already speaking out against it. To select this new group of "religious leaders," the Universal Pix crew headed straight for that hot bed of religious leftists in New York City at 475 Riverside Drive. This high rise structure, also known as "The God Box" or "Heaven on the Hudson," houses headquarters for the World Council of Churches, the National Council of Churches, and a host of other left leaning and not-so-left leaning religious structures. U. P. people were smart enough to know that this address could be counted upon to cough up any number of clerics who would be most likely to tolerate or even support a film rewriting the narrative of the biblical Jesus. After all, this was the locus for the Angela Davis Defense Fund which, years ago, was foisted on a number of mainline denominations and was partly responsible for splitting the Presbyterian Church. Since the press doesn't have a category known as "leftists," these people were referred to in media reports as "moderates." They are about as moderate in the world of orthodox Christianity as Fidel Castro is moderate in the world of democracy.

We knew, also, that there would be a bevy of those attending this well-announced, but closely guarded, screening who would walk out of the theater at about four o'clock New York time into well-positioned microphones and cameras. They would be saying things like "*The Last Temptation of Christ* is a deeply spiritual experience," "It is a masterful portrait of Christ even as the gospels are portraits of Christ," or "I am asking *all* my parishoners to see it *at least* once to share in its majestic beauty and inspirational grandeur." When that happened, it would be *no* surprise to those of us who revere the accurate, eyewitness portrayals of Christ and His ministry in the New Testament Gospels.

Ever since the conference call involving the "offended brethren"--Dobson, Bright, Ogilvie, Hayford, Wildmon--there had been talk of putting together some kind of press conference. We felt we had to take our story into the marketplace, and we had to do it in a way that would give us the advantage of both mass and surprise. If we waited until Universal's religious spokespersons hit the national press with their predictable palaver about the film's "artistic merit," we knew we would be playing catch-up ball again, a position Christians always seem to occupy.

A second conference call, a lot of additional prayer, and some more strategizing resulted in a plan that felt comfortable to all of us.

* A press conference involving as many of the Southern California members of the "offended brethren" as possible

* A prepared statement for the press outlining what Universal had done and was intending to do with the film and our

75

request of them not to release it

* A location for the conference that would be classy, easily accessible to the press, and boldly situated on Universal's doorstep

* A timing that would get our story to the national press before the statements from those exiting the New York screening got to them

* A call for a response from Universal that would put *them* on the defensive for a change

Few of us had ever put together a press conference! I had never even *attended* one!

As we talked among the Key Men as to who had some experience with press conferences, the name of a seasoned Hollywood journalist and former Vice President for Public Affairs at NBC came up. He knew the press and he knew press conferences. He had set up hundreds of them, so one of the Key Men approached him. After asking a lot of tough questions about the purpose and composition of the conference, he said he would be glad to help. Great! But we had only *two working days* to set it up!

I freed up two Mastermedia staff guys who moved into a Burbank office on Monday, July 11, to try to set up the conference for Tuesday, July 12! Working from a list of press people in Southern California, these two guys spent all day on the phone calling the media.

When we had decided that The Registry hotel on the

Universal Studios lot was the place to hold the conference, my business manager checked on a room and learned that they had no small rooms available-- only a part of the ballroom. Basically, we wanted a small room for two reasons: (1) If only a half dozen press people showed up, they wouldn't rattle around in the room like a BB in a box car, and (2) a small room would have a small price! We were willing to go a couple of hundred dollars, but the ballroom was an "exorbitant" $750 plus the cost of catering the coffee! We told The Registry we'd "get back to them ."

You have to understand. This press conference was being funded by religious *ministries!* Despite the image portrayed by recent scandals in televangelism, most ministries don't have money. My tongue-in-cheek explanation as to why there isn't more embezzlement in churches and Christian ministries is that there is little inducement to abscond with a *deficit!* I am convinced, based on my twenty-five year record of personal investing and observing the investments of other ministers, that most clergymen are predestined by God to be "non-profit." I'm sure that too much involvement with the temporal dulls one's commitment to the eternal and vice versa. For much of my quarter century in ministry, my organizations have operated hand to mouth.

Just as my business manager was beginning to look for a smaller (and cheaper) hotel room, I learned that Tim had already told someone from the media that the conference would be held at The Registry! Nice guy! We had no choice now but to confirm the room there. I figured I might have to put it on my personal credit card. I wasn't sure the ministry had the money for it. We'd have to trust God not to let the press rattle around in the room too much.

Once again there were four opinions--maybe five--for every three people. For example: "We can't get the press corps to attend a press conference on 24 hours notice!" "Anything organized on this short notice will look like a makeshift deal to the media pros." "What do we have to say to the press?" "Aren't we acting like lions entering a den of Daniels?" "What will keep us from being chewed up and spit out like every other Christian leader who faces the overwhelming majority of the irreligious in the media?"

A call from Donald Wildmon indicated his strong resistance to the idea of a press conference. He'd been chewed up and spit out by the press too many times. It wasn't a big problem for us if Donald wouldn't be with us, because we had determined that it would be best to have this be a "Southern California coalition." We also knew that Wildmon had played to extremely mixed reviews even among the more responsible members of the press community. Whether the controversial image was deserved or not, we wanted to launch whatever we launched with as little prejudgment from the media as possible.

Even Tim had hesitations about the timing of the press conference. We had some long discussions about the relative risks of different scenarios. I finally prevailed in convincing him that we had to get our statement to the press before Universal's hand picked clergy. We knew these grinning, "Joe Isuzu's of the cloth" would hit the streets and talk show circuits with their glib assurances they were providing the Gospel Truth. The press conference would provide our cause with the element of *surprise*.

Tim was easy to convince that, with the first *Hollywood Reporter* ad hitting the trades on Monday and the Dobson show hitting the Christian world the same day, it was imperative that we hit the secular press on Tuesday--the principle of *mass*. We felt that if God would give us favor, shots one and two might even pique the curiosity of the press sufficiently that they would come to the conference and then help us turn shot number three into a multiple warhead!

Furthermore, if Tim could lay that "word of the Lord" bit on me regarding the signatures on *The Hollywood Reporter* ad, this was one time I had that same, absolutely undeniable and inescapable conviction in my spirit that Tuesday was *God's* timing. I felt that I would wrong Him if I bowed to pressure for any other schedule.

The time was set for Tuesday at 10:00 a. m. in Ballroom C of The Registry hotel. Lloyd Ogilvie, Jack Hayford, and Bill Bright would join Tim and me. I would moderate the conference to give better attention to Tim and the Christian leaders. Tim was the key player in the game, and Bright, Hayford, and Ogilvie had tremendous respect in Southern California as both righteous and reasonable men. I was virtually unknown, but represented believers in the industry and the consultant role to Tim.

I worked on the press statement, and, after some telephone interaction with the others, put it in final form for the conference. The statement summarized the history of the relationship with Universal, the base of information for the attack on a film we had not personally seen, and outlined the objections of the "coalition:"

* The portrayal of Jesus Christ ". . . as a mentally deranged and lust-driven man who convinces Judas Iscariot to betray him, whose own mother, Mary, declares him crazy, who questions His powers and Messiahship, and, in a dream sequence, comes down off the cross and has a sexual relationship with Mary Magdalene . . ."

* Universal Pictures' violation of its written commitments to give a select group of Christian leaders a chance to pre-screen the film "far in advance of the release date," and the false representations made to the Christian community by declaring the movie to be a "reaffirmation of faith," and portraying Jesus "as sinless, as deity, and as the savior of mankind."

* Universal's decision to release the film to the public after months of paid counsel regarding its explosive potential for Christian backlash and its apparent motivation to set aside public responsibility for financial gain.

* The highly discriminatory nature of Universal's decision against the Christian community in view of its presumed unwillingness "to release a major film maligning the character and distorting the historical record of any other religious, ethnic, or national hero."

The statement called for Universal "to abandon its plans to release the movie" and asked "that the film be destroyed to prevent its future release or sale." It urged sympathizers to "take firm but responsible action against the corporation" in an effort to convince them that the film should not be shown.

There were some sleepless nights for a number of us between Friday, when the plan was hatched, and Tuesday. One of my Mastermedia staff men confessed later that he hardly slept thinking we were lighting a big bomb in our own laps by having the conference at all.

Again we prayed--individually and collectively--mostly on phone calls. We prayed for there to be a spirit of peace and tranquility from the moment the first press person entered the room. We asked God to give us favor with the press. We asked that there not be any disruption of the conference. We prayed for each member of the coalition and for guidance as to the words each would say. We asked God to order the sequence of questions from the media and to govern the "flow" of the conference content.

My staff team and I got to The Registry about forty-five minutes early. Ballroom C looked cavernous to me as a handful of media people were setting up way in the front end. Beautiful $750 an hour room, though! Nice chandeliers and all.

The members of the coalition were supposed to meet for final briefing and prayer at 9:30. Tim was on Pat Robertson's 700 Club program by satellite that morning launching the story to Pat's immense following. We expected Tim to arrive at any minute. The first person I met in the halls was Ken Wales, a Christian producer who had come to give us some moral support.

Drs. Bright, Ogilvie, and Hayford arrived and gathered in a side room with Tim and me at about 9:45, so there were rushed greetings, a super quick briefing, and a short time of prayer around the circle.

I felt like we were breaking from the huddle for the championship game as we strode next door to start the conference. Before Tim even got to the door, the *Entertainment Tonight* reporter stuck a mike, a camera and a bank of lights in his face. "We can't stay for the conference. You've got to give us a quote, anything, just a sound bite, anything." Shocked, Tim said something he doesn't remember into the cameras and proceeded with the rest of us toward the ballroom.

Even if I was a little psyched about the whole thing, as the butterflies in my mid-section indicated, nothing could have prepared me for what I saw as I stepped through the ballroom door. THE PLACE WAS FULL! There must have been 150 people in that room. There were thirteen cameras in the room and four vans with satellite dishes in the parking area outside. The sixty chairs that hotel catering had set up had already been supplemented. People, cameras, cords, lights, AV equipment, and note pads circled the gallery. I couldn't believe my eyes!

I breathed a quiet "Thank you, Lord!" as the members of the coalition took the dais. Microphones of every conceivable description were duct-taped to the podium and masking-taped to each other until the speaking desk seemed covered with metallic floral bouquets.

As I stepped to the rostrum to call the meeting to order, I noticed that there wasn't much disorder to call out. There was quiet conversation going on around the room that had already begun to hush before I spoke. In fact, there *was* a spirit of tranquility and peace in the room!

I introduced myself, made a quick "run through" of the house rules and read the prepared statement. Cameras whirred, pencils scratched, and this professional congregation was as attentive as any I have addressed in my own church. Finished with the call to order, I started down the table introducing the guests.

Tim Penland had drawn the pole position and stood up to speak, his broad shoulders and fastidiously groomed coat and tie bespeaking a man of stature as well as status. Still stunned by the ambush from the *Entertainment Tonight* crew, he began, his deep voice resonating with a brief extemporaneous statement. You could tell he was struggling to get his thoughts together. At that moment, Tim related later, a number of emotions struck him as never before--*grief* that it all had to end this way, *disappointment* that all attempts at reason with Universal had failed, and *uncertainty* over what this moment would mean for his future in the film business. Tim briefly expressed his "great concern" over the situation that had precipitated the conference and expressed hope that Universal would listen to the appeal and stop the release. He finished his remarks and sat down.

Dr. Bill Bright was vintage Dr. Bill Bright. Not an orator nor a logician in style, Bill fullfilled the role for which he is known best among the thousands of Campus Crusade for Christ staff worldwide--he gave witness to how Jesus Christ had changed his life. "I am a Christian," he began with precise declaration. He testified how, more than 40 years earlier as an agnostic businessman, he had studied the life of "the most perfect man who ever walked the face of the earth, the most loving, gracious, compassionate person." He told how he had "fallen in love with Christ." He told "how angry, how broken" he was when he attempted to read the script of *Temptation*. With deep emotion he spoke of "not having a good night's sleep in several weeks" since he had put down the script that defamed his precious Lord. As he peered over the stockpile of media microphones, he declared that out of obedience to God he would "love the men who created this terrible film."

Enter the national debating champ for the year who-knows-what, Dr. Jack Hayford. Stepping to the microphone, he spoke as if to state the opening case for the affirmative side on the resolution, "Resolved: Universal Pictures has perpetrated discrimination and injustice in its plans to produce and release *The Last Temptation of Christ.*" "Pastor Jack," as he is known with affection to the minions of media people who file through the doors of Church on the Way (more than through the doors of any other place of worship in California) laid it out straight. He pressed first on the "decency" which film makers have commonly afforded historical figures when presenting caricatures of them --changed names, and legal disclaimers regarding similarity of the caricature to the real person. Then, moving in powerfully to get as many points from the judges of this debate as possible, he called not for *favored* status for Christianity but for *equal* status. He declared that Universal studios had a "serious point of accountability to history and to the liberties all of us enjoy in this nation." Having supported the resolution, he took his seat.

Dr. Lloyd John Ogilvie--calling him just Lloyd Ogilvie

seems like disrespect for a man with such class and distinction--took the rostrum. He was his usual flawless self with distinct, deliberate articulation of well-fashioned thoughts. Pear-shaped tones, handsome good looks, and a Scottish pronunciation now and then made him a dead ringer for someone central casting might have provided to play the part of someone who could bring together the images of "Hollywood" and "Presbyterian." He declared that the film will "disturb and distort the life of Jesus for those who are thinking about Christianity, it will hurt and destroy those who have begun the Christian life, and it will add to the moral decay of our time in history." In one of the favorite lines clipped later by the media, he called *The Last Temptation of Christ* (read this slowly in your deepest voice) "The most serious misuse of filmcraft in the history of moviemaking."

I represented the hundreds of working professionals in film and television who are Christian--even inside the walls of Universal--who were and are even now being torn between allegiance to their Lord and Savior and loyalty to their companies and professions. I projected that perhaps 30% of Universal's 16,800 employees might be Christians caught in this untenable position. I indicated that a number of those working professionals had expressed themselves in *The Hollywood Reporter* ad calling for Universal not to release the film.

Even though his priorities would not permit him to be at the press conference, Dr. James Dobson's perspective was stated clearly that morning in the *Los Angeles Times.* The *Times* quoted him as saying, "It would appear to be the most blasphemous, evil attack on the Church and the cause of Christ in the history of entertainment. Universal and Scorsese are not merely taking on evangelicals; they are taking on the King of the universe. God is not mocked. I don't know how long it will take Him to speak, but He will speak."[12]

Open for questions.

Serious press people surfaced immediately. *Cable News Network*, *Time* , the *Los Angeles Times*, *People, USA Today, Entertainment Tonight*, the networks-- they all were there. They asked Dr. Ogilvie why he thought the film was "the most serious misuse of filmcraft" in movie making history. He told 'em. They asked how reasonable we thought it was to expect that Universal would decide not to release the film. We told them we believed in miracles, but that we also knew that Universal would have to deal with the financial and business realities of their decisions. They asked if this was censorship. We told them we had been *invited* to give input to the film by Universal and that we were making an appeal to decency, not calling for governmental or ecclesiastical pressure to prohibit the film's release.

Believe me, having no frame of reference with press conferences before, I thought the affair was going pretty well. The questions were tough but very fair. Censorship? Fiction? Boycott? Evidence? It was obvious that they were taking us seriously. It was obvious that the answers to the questions were striking home. It was obvious they were "into" the issues. It was obvious that they weren't leaving the hall to get to the next story!

A full fifty-five minutes into the press conference, I broke into the Q & A with the observation that we had intended to close the conference after an hour. Judging from the involvement, I queried, might they want to extend it a bit? Nobody moved. Nobody spoke. Nobody breathed. Nobody blinked. The corps was transfixed as if nobody had ever dared ask *them* a question? I broke the awkward silence with the comment, "I have never seen the press so quiet in my life" and, amid slight laughter, arbitrarily extended the time limit ten minutes.

As I was just about ready to "make it a wrap," as they say in the business, I remembered the wrinkled piece of paper that had been handed to me during the conference and had been jammed into one of my coat pockets. As the dialogue on one question continued, I found it and pulled it out. It read, "Larry, I just learned from one of the men here that it was in this same room less than a year a ago that Pope John Paul II called the leaders of media to responsibility in their professions. Lew Wasserman introduced him on that occasion. You might want to mention this." Dynamite!

When the time had expired, I thanked the media elite for their attendance and concluded. "It was the dream of seeing bridges built between the Christian community and Hollywood that led us into a relationship with Universal. That dream was proclaimed to leaders of the media in this very room less than a year ago by Pope John Paul II. On that occasion Lew Wasserman presided. Despite what has happened, we want you to know that that dream is still alive."

Adjournment. Press people cornering various individuals to have them eat their microphones. A cluster of people around me. An agressive woman who quickly, but unintentionally, betrayed that she was there on behalf of Universal. She slipped by referring to Universal as "we." She wanted to know who said, "The Christians can't stop us from releasing the film" as mentioned by one reporter and repeated by Bill Bright. I clarified that, from my understanding, it was not Tom Pollock as Dr. Bright had said, but Sid Sheinberg. More interviews. The room emptied. It was over.

More accurately, it was *begun*. The last of the three missile shots had hit their targets within thirty hours. We'd have to wait for the fallout from the blast to clear to see how much ground could be claimed.

Back at command central, we began to get reports from the battlefield. One public relations pro said, "We used to measure the success of a press conference by the number of camera heads. We had thirteen. Never been to a press conference with more." Another said, "The thing that stunned me was the attention. Usually after fifteen to twenty minutes the reporters have their statements and footage and are packing off to the next story. Not here. Larry, do you realize that they stayed for AN HOUR AND FIVE MINUTES?" How would that impress me? I told you this was my *first* press conference.

A network veep opined, "Larry, I have never witnessed nor heard tell of a press conference in which the press gave the participants an ovation at the end of it!"

"Did they?" I asked myself. "I guess they did, didn't they." The video of the event recorded rather sustained applause . . . by the *press!*

I was skeptical about the results. Too many times I had left an interview with a reporter feeling that it had gone very well only to read the copy and realize they had made chopped liver of me and my position. Would this be different?

A lot of things were different over the next few days. It was clear that a number of incredible things were beginning to happen. A report:

Missile One: *The Hollywood Reporter* Ad

After the initial ambivalence by Christians in media over being asked to identify publicly (a) with Christ and (b) with a request of a film company not to release a film defaming Him, the community settled out into two rather clear camps. Those who made the decision to sign the ad started a contagious and enthusiastic campaign to get others to do so. At this writing 161 have had their names appear in the trades with many more having given permission. The second group, those that decided not to do so, found excuses--some excellent, some flaky--but still excuses. A few had good, respectable reasons.

The appearance of those names became talk all over town. Charles Cappleman, Vice President for Operations at CBS Television City, found that much of CBS seemed to know of his decision, even at Black Rock, CBS' corporate headquarters in New York. Jimmie Baker, a forty year veteran producer with ABC who signed the ad, got to the studio to find the ad posted on the bulletin boards. Richard Kiel, the 7'4" steel mouthed "Jaws" in the James Bond movies, signed the ad and "considered it a privilege to stand up for his Lord." Fred Waugh, a leading Hollywood stunt man who coordinated the stunts on the award winning movie *Shoot to Kill* and who climbed the outside of the Empire State Building years ago as Spiderman, not only signed the ad but recruited other stunt people to sign as well.

A man who captured the spirit of the ad best was John Carroll, President of Continental Camera, an aerial support company to film makers in the *Airwolf* TV series, *Out of Africa, Top Gun*, and other top films. John prayed with me over lunch at the Van Nuys airport restaurant to place his faith in Jesus Christ in March of 1987. When asked about signing his name to the ad, he said, "After all Jesus Christ has done for me in only *one year* of knowing Him personally, how could I do anything less than take this stand for Him?" Less than 30 days after the ad appeared, John went to see his Beloved Friend when a heart attack took him at the poolside of his residence. His unsolicited contribution check for the cause arrived at our office after he was gone.

Through no manipulation whatever, the list had surnames from virtually every ethnic and racial minority. A sprinkling of Jewish believers (known often as "messianic Jews") gave their names to the ad.

The ad was such a stunner to the media community that the *Los Angeles Times* reprinted the ad as part of an article in the Calendar section. Though reduced in size, the name reproduction was so clear that every name of the valiant "initial sixty-one" could be read perfectly.

That was exciting to every name on the list but one--a guy with the same name as one of the signators to the ad. He called "steamed" because he did not want to be identified with Christ or the appeal to Universal. He kept repeating "but that's *my* name!" We agreed to run a classifed ad in the *Hollywood Reporter* stating that the John Doe in the ad was not the John *S.* Doe in the entertainment business!

Missile Two: the James Dobson Program

Response from Christians nationwide was so overwhelming that a flood of protest inundated Universal. By the beginning of office time on Monday, July 11, the flood of calls from East Coast people who had heard the program as much as three hours earlier was clogging Universal's phone lines. Many couldn't get an open line for days. Within a few days the phone system was barely operable. While the Black Tower is not talking about the volume of either phones calls or letters, an early insider report was that they had more than 10,000 a day from July 12 on. Insiders also reported that doing business was barely possible because even calls inside the studio lot were affected. This pressure was aided by believers in Christ working for Universal who called and gave us directory listings and, when the numbers were changed to solve the problem, called saying, "They just changed the numbers again. I called thinking you might want to have them!"

While we have no idea how many pieces of mail *The Last Temptation* Gang received, an inside report indicated that on *one day* three or four weeks after the first press conference they received 122,000 letters. Dr. Dobson's office was running 4,000 to 5,000 calls a day for a number of days after the broadcast from people across America requesting Fact Sheets, seeking to get involved, and complaining because they could never get a line open into Universal. The Dobson organization eventually handled more than 25,000 calls! Banks of operators were put on at the Black Tower, and one report said many of them didn't last more than four hours. That was a tough job, having to defend Universal's decision to defame Christ as fast as you could lift the phones.

One of the significant facts of the campaign that the press has chosen to ignore is the sheer *numbers* of calls and letters Universal has received! Despite our challenge to a number of eager journalists to extract from Universal management, from the phone company, or from the postal substations what the numerial volume of this protest was, not *one* of the hundreds covering this story ever pursued it. It was as if they really did not want to know.

Missile Number Three: The Press Conference

There was no doubt but that missile number three had made a direct hit. We got enormous and immediate coverage. Ours was the lead story on many TV and radio news programs and front page on many of the major dailies. Associated Press and United Press International beamed the story nationwide. Even papers in London gave us coverage. And, wonder of wonders, I don't know of one story that was of the "stick-it-to-'em" variety from that press conference! God had graciously given us favor with the press. We were represented fairly . . . but not for long!

The real proof that this missile was a perfect bullseye was Universal's response. From inside the Black Tower a secretary told us of the utter pandemonium that reigned--cursing, blaming, arguing execs trying to figure out what hit them. Long and desperate "crisis control" meetings turned into shouting matches. Cadres of attorneys followed every move lest the pressure from outside the moat take litigious form.

The situation outside the walls gave even more convincing proof of the direct hit. Imagine this, a three and half billion dollar media giant with prides of roaring PR and press relations people who *daily* feed the press, court the press, massage the press, and manipulate the press--WOULDN'T TALK TO THE PRESS! A friend who is a field reporter for NBC news called me and said, "Larry, NBC wants to do a story, but we *can't get any pictures!* In TV we have to have pictures, and Universal is operating under a *siege mentality*. We can't get clips. We can't get statements. We can't get interviews. We have never seen anything like this! We can't believe this is Universal!"

Surprise and *mass* combined to gain the first major victory under the masterful coordination of whom? A handful of ministers and media consultants? Get serious. The biggest laugh we had from the articles coming out of the three missile barrage was the wording of the first line of a front page story in *Variety:*

> If the wrath of God does not fall on Universal
> studios, the wrath of God's well organized,
> media savvy armies will.[13]

Who? Us? This was a last minute, patched-together effort by an unstructured, assorted, for-want-of-a-better-word "coalition" of people who happen to believe that God is not dead. We *know* He is alive and lives in Hollywood. We all talked to Him this morning. We said "Thank you, Father!"

6

The Empire Strikes Back

It was sweet while it lasted. It just didn't last long. You couldn't expect the gang in the deep carpet area of MCA/Universal to keep the drawbridge up forever. And you can be sure the big boys were consuming dramatically greater quantites of midnight oil while it was up! It stayed up for about four days.

We would have given a lot to be a fly on the wall in some of those executive jam sessions, but we can't complain about the information we got regularly from the people inside. Although on *not one single occasion* did we ever make a request for confidential information from a believer (or an unbeliever) inside Universal, we got a steady flow. This seems to me to be mute testimony to the fact that one's loyalty to the One who has provided forgiveness, hope, power, peace, joy, and eternal life transcends all other loyalties.

We also never encouraged disloyalty to Universal leadership from Christian employees. Even in our widely distributed Fact Sheet we counseled employees only to *expressions of conviction* and *resignation* -- never disobedience, strikes, slowdowns, disloyalties, or abuse.

About ten days after the press conference, I got a call from a young man working on the Universal lot. "Dr. Poland," he began, "There are a number of groups of Christians that work here, and we are very upset about what our company is doing. We are going to be meeting over lunch today, and it was suggested that I call to get counsel as to what we should do. Can you tell us?"

"I'll try. But, first, I think I should tell you what *not* to do. I have been in management for twenty-five years, and I know what I don't like as a manager and what the Bible says not to do. Okay if I start there?"

"Sure."

"Okay. No petitions, no log rolling, no threats, and no mass efforts. For those under authority these activities are counterproductive, they alienate supervisors, and they are in violation of the biblical model for dealing with the authority relationship you have with your employer. Instead, pass the word to the other believers to go to their supervisors *individually* and *privately*. Explain respectfully to your supervisor that you are a Christian and that the film that is coming out of Universal is deeply offensive to you. Explain that this decision by management is forcing you to choose between your loyalty to God and to your employer. Ask your supervisor to pass the word up the line that you view this with great seriousness and you wish to request that the company not discriminate against you and your beliefs. If supervisors all over the lot are passing the word up the line, they will get the message. What they do with it is their responsibility."

"That's pretty much what we were thinking should be our approach. Thank you for confirming it."

We ended the phone calls with pleasant and mutual "God bless you's."

Things at the executive level of the Big U. were not so pleasant, however. After being stunned, as they were, by the first three missile strikes, they poured themselves into a counteroffensive. The drawbridge began to lower a bit by the fifth day. Pollock granted an interview to Pat Broeske, one of Universal's not-so-favorite people and "Calendar" editor of the *Los Angeles Times*. In the interview he made sharp comments about Martin Scorsese. He made sure the readers knew this was *Scorsese's* film, that *Scorsese* was the one who would have to interpret the movie's theological message, that it was *Scorsese's* failure to have the film ready that caused Universal to miss the screening for the conservative Christian leaders.

Anyone who bought all of that would be a great candidate for joining the Nebraska navy, but it was apparent what was happening inside the Ebony Turret. The buck that had been dropped on Pollock's desk by Lew Wasserman was now being thrown bitterly into Scorsese's lap. The next indication that the film was being exiled from Universal City was when Marian Billings, Scorsese's personal New York publicist, was put in charge of publicity for the whole film! When Filmdom's corporate giant delegates responsibility for publicity on the highest publicity risk film in its history to a director's publicist, you know one of two things: it is eager to distance itself from it, or Alzheimer's disease has set in.

Evidence coming from the headquarters during the next few days and weeks gave no evidence that the leadership had lost its mental faculties. Questionable motives can coexist with mental acuity! To help you get a feel for the people behind the corporate mask, I am providing here a summary of some of the corporate players and the dynamics that came to play during the following days. While I cannot, for obvious reasons, document most of this material. there is no question about the trustworthiness of the sources that provided it. You must be warned, however, that, while this section is based on information believed to be reliable, it does involve conjecture on our part. No doubt some of the specific thoughts, motivations, responsibilities, and quotes are inaccurate, but for obvious reasons we can't confirm these things with those involved!

****

Lew Wasserman, MCA Chairman

Lew Wasserman, generally recognized to be the most powerful man in film and TV, is a 75 year old, superficially benign individual who has an immense instinct for power and for a "deal." I say *superficially* benign because his gentlemanly manner and somewhat quiet approach belie an ability to "go for the jugular" when he has set his sights on a goal and something or someone is in his way. *U. S. News and World Report* and *Forbes Magazine* both list his personal net worth at over 225 million dollars. He is charming in manner and is socially and financially well connected internationally. Lew is accustomed to getting what he wants.

Up to a point Wasserman was blindsided by *The Last Temptation* deal. Because his management style is to demand high accountability of his managers, but to let them work without tight control or restraint, he was only superficially aware of the deal with Scorsese and the creation of this movie. In addition, he was in Europe for a month while this thing was heating up and arrived back in town just a few days before before the July 12 press conference. He had not read a script nor seen any part of the film as of the week of July 4.

When he started getting the heat on personal calls from long time friends, he was, to say the least, not pleased. He began to take the situation personally and determined to get to the bottom of it. Shortly thereafter, in a high level meeting, he ordered, as only Lew Wasserman can order, "Get this film out of here! I've got a business to run!" Lew Wasserman has been confronted by some of the most powerful men and women in America with the request to kill the film -- influential neighbors, old time media friends, Archbishop Roger Mahoney of Los Angeles, Washington and Sacramento legislators, and a number of heads of major U. S. corporations. He also has been confronted by some of the lowliest. His chauffer, for example, turned quietly in his seat one day and addressed his boss with one line, "Mr. Wasserman, I wouldn't want to be in your shoes on judgment day."

Sid Sheinberg, MCA President

Sid Sheinberg lacks Wasserman's polish. While they share a high value on money and power, Sheinberg has a reputation for being tough, out of control with his anger at times, and verbally coarse and abusive. In one executive meeting Sheinberg reportedly railed against Christians and, with curses and denunciations, generally made a scene. Wasserman, having heard enough, told him to keep quiet, that he wanted to hear no more of it. Many with experience working with (or against) Universal executives feel that Sheinberg and Garth Drabinsky, head of Cineplex Odeon, are the tough cookies of the MCA/Universal/Cineplex Odeon empire.

Sheinberg undoubtedly was more aware of the Scorsese/*Last Temptation* deal than Wasserman, but, as president of the parent company, Sheinberg was not the key player. Probably nothing that happens involving LTOC will touch his job. He is entrenched. Even if MCA is bought out in a takeover, Sheinberg's "golden parachute" would catch 14 million dollars for him. Not bad for a man who wears MCA's black hat!

Tom Pollock, Chairman, Universal Pictures

Pollock is the guy on the hot seat in *The Last Temptation* fiasco. The deal with Scorsese was his, the approval for Scorsese to do this film was his, and the packaging of the deal was largely his. Within four days after the July 12 press conference Wasserman's office was making it clear to all concerned that Tom Pollock was handling this one. Wasserman was trying to distance himself from this movie monster. He told Pollock that he had gotten them into this deal and he was going to get them out. Insiders are not giving very high odds that Pollock will survive this mess with his job. Any way you look at it, Pollock has the most to lose personally and professionally by his association with *Temptation.* One report suggests that the September "resignation" of Universal's director of distribution, William Soady, was a precursor of the "alumni" status soon to befall Pollock. The *Los Angeles Times* later indicated that Soady's resignation was indeed a firing at the hands of Pollock.

****

The corporate counteroffensive now began. As we had expected, there was a slight delay before they hit the streets, but by July 16 the clergymen from the New

York screening were out in full force. Talk shows were abuzz with previously unheard of men of the cloth saying *The Last Temptation of Christ* was a "wonnnnnderful experience."

New York Episcopal Bishop Paul Moore was describing the film as "artistically excellent and theologically sound."[14] Andrea Cano, communications officer for the U. S. office for the World Council of Churches, suggested the film would lend itself nicely for use in churches as a videocassette with study guides. Rev. Charles Bergstrom, Chairman of Norman Lear's People for the American Way executive committee, said he was "not offended in any way Scripture was used and applied."[15] Rev. David Pomeroy, minister in the United Church of Christ and media representative with the National Council of Churches, was quoted by John Lofton in the *Washington Times* as saying, "Yes, the film does depict Christ in a sexual relationship with Mary Magdalene, but it was *tastefully done* [emphasis added]."[16] Dr. James Dobson responded to that statement with an incredulous "Heaven help us!"

What the uncritical viewer seldom stops to ask is, "Who do these guys represent?" Pick a viewpoint, any viewpoint and, with a little time, I can roust out at least a handful of guys with backward collars to support it. In most cases I won't have to go more than fifty miles. A man of the cloth for homosexuality? Easy. There are a number of homosexual churches and an organization called "Born Again Gays." A procommunist pastor? No sweat. Latin America and many parts of the U.S. have a heavy spinkling of "liberation theology" proponents. Want a minister who doesn't want the President of the United States to encourage the reading of the Bible? I can get you a

Unitarian from Los Angeles. Pick a doctrinal abberation, any abberation, and you surely will find some "Christian minister" from the First Unorthodox Church of Sheepsclothing to espouse it.

Then, out of nowhere, came Robert Thompson, a good looking young minister to a small, American Baptist flock in Evanston, Illinois. Robert showed up on the CBS morning show to "debate" the film with Tim Penland even though Tim had made it clear in accepting the CBS invitation that he would *not* debate a minister who had seen the film because he was not a minister. He told CBS he would come *only* if he could answer questions about his role with Universal. Not until he was *on the show with Thompson* did Tim realize that CBS was going to put him up against a minister and make a debate out of it despite its promises!

Robert projected his position with an intensity that seemed slightly overdone to be raw sincerity. His eyes seemed to have a kind of inexplicable terror behind them not completely attributable to stage fright. They didn't smile when his mouth did.

Thompson took two approaches in defending the film, one direct and one indirect. The direct approach was tough to handle coming, at that time, from one of fewer than forty people on the face of the globe outside the production company who had seen the film. The approach was, essentially, "But have you *seen* the film?" At that time all any of us could say was, "No, but I have read two versions of the script, have information from an unnamed source inside Universal, and . . . ." But it really didn't seem to make any difference what you said after you said, "No . . . ." The "select few" would stick you with powerful lines like

"Well, if you had *seen* the film . . ." or "How can you speak against a film you *haven't seen?*"

Thompson's indirect approach was exactly what my illprepared undergraduate students of college sociology used to use on essay exams. We called it *snow*. A working definition of snow, Thompson style, might be "Any delightful sounding, well articulated non-content you can generate to avoid answering a direct question."

An example from the CBS dialogue:

Penland:

> As powerful as the film medium is . . . a scene of the last supper where Jesus and some of the disciples are breaking bread, and you see blood and flesh dripping from the mouths of the apostles. Is that a scene he wants to implant in the minds of his congregation forever?

Thompson:

> That's the artistic *genius* I'm talking about! It is precisely the fact that one cannot view this film *literally*. One must view it as a *symbol*, as something that represents a reality and a truth that *transcends* the images on the screen.

There is no way of telling how the viewers were secured for the New York screening. But Robert Thompson's access to it from the north suburbs of Chicago is no mystery. While Tim was in Universal's employ, Robert Thompson called him and, in a somewhat strange conversation, bemoaned the fact that the evangelicals, the Christian conservatives, always got to the heart of the action. He wondered aloud how that happened and why the liberals always seemed to be on the outside looking in. Maybe, he mused, it was just because they were not so well organized. Later Thompson called Universal requesting to be included in a screening because he wanted to help them counteract the fundamentalists. I speculate that Pollock and Co. had to reflect on that request about 2 or 3 milliseconds before they granted him a pass to New York!

The outcome of the CBS show was pretty balanced between Robert and Tim, but I went crazy watching the program from my family room when, for the umpteenth time, the interviewer's *first question* was, "Have you seen the film?" and Tim had to respond truthfully that he hadn't. I had had it. We *had* to figure out some parry that could answer that predictable first thrust. We had to tell 'em we had seen the script and had been familiar with the content for months. We had to tell 'em we hadn't seen Jesus, either, but we knew what He was like, because He had changed our lives. We had to tell 'em most judges and juries haven't seen the crime they're judging, but they have *reliable evidence*. We had to think of *something* we could say besides "No."

It was really pretty silly, my going through these theatrics alone with my TV set while Robert Thompson sat there uttering nice sounding vagaries. It was just so maddening that, even though there were excellent and cogent answers to the "Have you seen . . ." question, none of them had the power of saying "Yes, I have!" And every time we had to say "No" and the other guy could say "Yes" it was catch up ball again. I *hate* catch up ball!

The parade of liberals from the New York screening were now flooding the talk shows and press interviews. I began to hear the people in the street and not a few people in the pew saying, "Well, maybe we have overreacted. I saw a minister on TV saying he thought the film was just fine!"

It wasn't enough that the New York screening contingent was going around the country saying, "But they haven't *seen* the film." The people of the press picked up the chant, too. Every article describing our stance included the line " . . . protesting a film they haven't seen." Soon it was as if we were in the middle of a great stadium squaring off with the opposition with a hundred thousand spectators in the stands cheering, "You haven't seen the film! You haven't seen the film! You haven't seen the film!"

I can understand the appeal of this chide. In nearly every film released to the public the viewer has absolutely no knowledge of what is in the film beyond the previews or clips carefully released by the production company. We never could get across that this film was different. The book on which the film was based had been around for a quarter of a century, Tim and I had access to the content of the script from Universal for some time, we had the reports from an eyewitness even before the New York screening and two from it, and a second script was floating around the country in quantities numbering in the thousands. How many films do you know that have had that much information circulating about them *prior to release?*

Even though Scorsese ridiculed the widely circulated script as being a five year old version, it varied from the final release (even allowing for some last minute

Scorsese edits) by less than 10%! Knowing we had solid evidence, it galled us every time we heard "But you haven't *seen* the film!" Even Paul Schrader later admitted the script we had was his but for two scenes!

Another main line of attack by *Temptation* defenders and the liberal press was to scream "fundamentalists!" every time they treated the story of any criticism or protest. These people, who would get dyspeptic if you called them "commies," "pinkos," "left wing radicals," or "pagans" resorted to calling virtually everybody that opposed the film "fundamentalists," or "the religious right." If it hadn't been such a violation of responsible journalism, it would have been hilarious.

Even after the national protest included Mother Teresa, the National Catholic Conference, the Eastern Orthodox Church, and selected Jewish and Muslim groups, you were told that the film was "being criticized by a group of fundamentalists." The irony of all this was that some of the people protesting the film would have been just as angry at being called fundamentalists as they were about the film. I got so tired of having TV producers put a tag line on head shots of me that said, "Fundamentalist Minister." I doubt if most of those who tried to dump this protest into the fundamentalist camp would know enough about the religious community to give you a good working definition of a fundamentalist. It was a blatant propaganda technique, but it had appeal: ". . . *fundamentalists who haven't seen the film*." Saying it lumped everybody in the national movement with fallen televangelists, red necks, white robed wierdos, and unthinking bigots.

A third approach was to scream "censorship!" We dealt with this question in the first press conference in detail: "Isn't this an attempt at censorship?" I wish I had a dollar for every time I had to give a liberal press person a freshman course in what censorship is. *Censorship is any governmental, ecclesiastical, or institutional prior restraint on content intended for public release, publication, or distribution.* I'll share the course outline with you.

1. We are violent enemies of censorship! When any governmental, ecclesiastical, or institutional body wants prior approval of content, *we in the religious community get censored first and worst.*

2. We are not forcing ourselves into Universal's First Amendment rights by expressing our views on this film. We were *invited in* by Universal to give input on the film as consultants and Christian leaders! *They asked us for input and got it!*

3. We are not interfering in Universal's right to produce or release any kind of trash they want. They've proved over and over they will exercise that right. This is an *appeal* to conscience, to morality, to nondiscrimination, to sensitivity, to respect, to human dignity.

4. We are not *restraining* movie goers from seeing any film they jolly well please. If the film is released, they are free to see it a hundred times if they wish.

5. Why is it that *our* public expression of views is a *violation* of First Amendment rights and *their* public expression is not? In view of the fact that the First Amendment has never in two hundred years been held to protect libel, slander,

106

defamation of character, or obscenity, this film is a whole lot closer to a violation of the First Amendment than our expressions are.

But no matter what we said in response to the cry of "censorship!" the media usually didn't report it. They just screamed it louder!

I don't remember hearing any of those "censorship!" cries when the Gay Media Task Force pressured film and TV companies to portray sodomites in a favorable light and set up an operation to evaluate scripts that deal with gay themes. They maintain an operation which *"edits" these scripts for networks and producers!* I guess "pressuring and editing" on one end is "intimidating and censoring" on the other. It was a triple whammy: " . . . *fundamentalists who haven't seen the film* are endeavoring to *censor* it."

It was working. For nearly a week after the Black Tower drawbridge came down The International Brotherhood of Universal Supporters hammered us on talk shows and in the press with the triple whammy. It began to smart, especially since we knew this was a smokescreen to hide the real issues.

At a time when our cause didn't need any other problems, we had two other setbacks on top of the lost ground in the media. One was my fault and one wasn't. In a letter to the Mastermedia mailing list I had attributed the quote, "The Christians aren't going to stop us from releasing this film" to Tom Pollock. Tim called me one day and said, "Larry, I just got off the phone with Pat Broeske of the *Los Angeles Times*. She somehow got a copy of the letter you sent to your mailing list attributing that 'The Christians aren't going to stop us . . .' quote to Tom Pollock. She asked Pollock if he said it, and he said he never said any such thing. Didn't you know it was Sid Sheinberg who said that?"

"Well, you know, Tim, I guess I have been confused on that."

"No, Larry. It was Sheinberg. I am certain I never told you anything else. I got the impression from Pat Broeske that Pollock was really angered by your doing that."

"I guess he had a right to be, if he didn't say it. I'd better call Pat right now and resolve the matter."

My heart sank. At a time when it seemed the tide was coming back in, I wasn't excited about making a public apology, but I knew that was the responsible thing to do.

I called Pat Broeske. "Pat, Tim Penland called and told me you had talked to Tom Pollock and that he denied ever making any statement like the one I attributed to him in my Mastermedia letter. I am really embarrassed about that and want you to know that I plan to make an apology to Tom asking his forgiveness. That was really careless of me to do that. If one of you people in the press did that, we'd really nail you wouldn't we?"

"Yes, I'm sure you would. What was the origin of the quote?"

"In checking my source, I confirmed that the statement was made by a Universal executive."

"Do you want to identify the person who said it? I thought at the press conference you had indicated that it was Sheinberg."

"No, I don't want to attribute it to anybody at this time, okay?"

"Okay, I'll just say the statement was made by another executive you declined to name."

"Fine. I really appreciate your handling of this. For the record, Tom Pollock will have an apology on his desk within 24 hours."

We terminated the call and I sat down at my word processor. I keyed in an unequivocal apology letter to Mr. Pollock asking for his forgiveness. I sent it off registered mail the next morning. The next day a *Times* headline read, "Temptation": Who Said What?" A caption read, "Evangelical Larry Poland says he'll seek Pollock's forgiveness."

That setback was *my* fault. The next one wasn't.

The next setback was named Rev. R. L. Hymers, Jr. Filling the vacuum for pictures faced by the TV news people was the pastor of a Los Angeles fundamentalist church (Yes, it actually has "fundamentalist" in its official name!) who decided to do a couple of things: (1) take some of his parishoners to Universal and to Lew Wasserman's home to hold dramatic protests, (2) focus on his imagined anti-Jewish backlash if the film were released. He unintentionally did a third: draw attention away from the real issues.

His strange tactics --having bloody Jesus actors

carrying crosses, an airplane pulling a sign over Wasserman's house declaring "Wasserman Fans Jew Hatred with Temptation," an actor portraying Lew Wasserman nailing spikes into Jesus' hands on a wooden cross--were live theater. But the factor that made them doubly live was Hymer's difficulty with anger management--nuclear explosions of focused ill will toward the unsuspecting. He screamed denunciations. He pounded his fists. He had shouting matches with anyone he chose. He engaged in unkind name calling. He stormed off the set of two TV shows. It was heartbreaking coming from a Christian brother.

In those critical days after Universal mounted its first counteroffensive, Rev. Hymers set the image of the protest back light years. Our hearts sank. We were struggling to shake off the phoney "fundamentalist" tag tied on us by the media. We were trying to project an image of reasoned, articulate, broad-based concern and were losing some media ground doing it. Then this guy blows on the scene from one of the few churches in Southern Cal with "fundamentalist" in its name and holds rallies at Universal Studios and Wasserman's home in a swank neighborhood inflaming anti-semitic passions and making every TV news clip of the protest.

If it wasn't so clear that *Hymers* was definitely his own man, we would have taken seriously one local network producer's half-serious suggestion that Universal had put him up to bizarre antics to discredit us! But I wonder if they could have concocted fiction that was so effective for their cause as this reality was! Hymers must be held largely responsible for lowering the level of the media's perception of the protest to a plateau from which it never ascended. He was so constantly visible that he became the image of the protest for much of America--not Penland, Poland, Dobson, Ogilvie, Bright, Hayford, Mahoney, or a host of other more restrained persons--Rev. Hymers.

Need I say that the morale in our ranks was rotten for nearly a week after the drawbridge at MCA came down? We were kicking our chins. Tinseltown's evil empire had struck back. And the way they struck back made it look like the "dark side of the force" was with them.

7

Buyout Proposal

During the turbulent days surrounding these events, those of us at the center of the storm were also trying to ride a see-saw of good and bad news. Our spirits were *up* when we heard that major theater chains had announced they wouldn't screen the film. We were *down* when more liberal Christian leaders announced they thought the film was great. We were *up* when we heard that key people inside Universal had gone on record with their company as opposing the film. We were *down* when we heard of Scorsese's coming out into the press to defend his film. We were *up* when we heard of an MCA/Universal stockholder revolt being planned. We were *down* when it seemed that few religious leaders were speaking out. We wanted off this see-saw!

It seemed that one important *defensive* strategy was to try to distance ourselves and the nationwide protest from Rev. Hymers' style of protest. At the peak of Hymers' media coverage Tim and I prayed one morning that God would give us a way to distance ourselves from him. Doing so was a tight rope act because Hymer's *was* on our side of the war, he *was* a brother in Christ, and he *was*, we still believe, well intentioned. But we had to get at least one hemisphere away from his "anti-semitic backlash" theme, his tasteless demonstrations, and his poorly managed ire--manifestations that seemed to get worse rather than better as time went on.

God answered that prayer the very day we prayed. I had turned down all the other TV stations in the Los Angeles market in their requests for on camera interviews because they weren't the right media settings for us to get our story across. I did agree to accept Channel 13's invitation, however, because I trusted the host of their "Top Story" segment, Larry Attebery. Larry was going to beam me live from my home for an interview with him in the studio. The crew arrived, set up their microwave link, and wired me for sound awaiting the "Top Story" segment of the ten o'clock news.

The station ran a short video clip to set up the segment after which Attebery began his introduction to the live segment with the words, "Live in our studios in Hollywood we have *Rev. R. L. Hymers* . . . and live from his home in Redlands, Dr. Larry Poland."

My blood ran cold. I had been ambushed! There was no way I would have agreed to be on the same program with Rev. Hymers! Could Attebery not know that? When the camera showed my face, I was ashen. I was angry and unnerved. I had to hold Channel 13 accountable for this!

After a short response by Hymers to one of Attebery's questions, I had my opportunity: "While I am sure there must be some areas of common ground between Rev. Hymers and myself," I intoned in as casual a manner as I could muster, "I'm very concerned about the generation of heat rather than light on the situation. Until this moment I had no idea that he was going to be on this program."

Hymers scowled. Hymers fumed. Hymers exploded at me, "Well, I wasn't told I was going to be on with you, either, and I don't like what you're saying!" The rest of the interaction was a textbook case in contrasts. Anyone thinking that Hymers and we were taking the same approach to the protest by the end of the program didn't have optic or auditory nerves! Thankfully, we attained some distance, but Hymers stayed in the spotlight.

But gaining distance was a *defensive* strategy. We needed to regain the *offensive!* We conferred, and we strategized. What language could we talk that Universal would understand? We all knew that the language Hollywood talks is "Dollarese." Legal tender is at one and the same time, Tinseltown's leading dialect and its supreme deity.

Those uninitated in the world of movies and television can seldom appreciate fully the omnipotence money has over every decision, every business matter, most lives, many relationships, and much of what passes for morality. The New Testament writer could have been standing on Sunset Boulevard, driving through Beverly Hills, or walking the Malibu beach when he wrote:

> But people who long to be rich soon begin to do all kinds of wrong things to get money, things that hurt them and make them evil-minded and finally send them to hell itself. For the love of money is the first step toward all kinds of sin. Some people have even turned away from God because of their love for it, and as a result have pierced themselves with many sorrows.
>
> I Timothy 6:9-10 LB

Paul, the wise rabbi and apostle who penned this statement to young Timothy, most assuredly could have written this sitting in a business meeting at a movie studio. While it is no secret that money has a prime role in commerce of any kind, those who have operated in the high echelons of the business world both inside and outside the world of media attest to the fact that when money is involved in Hollywood, it is perfectly appropriate to "*rise above* principle."

The chairman of the board of the Circle K convenience store empire, Karl Eller, served a short stint as President of Columbia Pictures after David Begelman was given the gate for a series of scandalous financial dealings. Eller described to me on one occasion the extent to which lying, broken contracts, exploitation, power tactics, conspiracies, and other violations of generally accepted business ethics were "the way things worked" in Hollywood. Eller couldn't get out of the movie business fast enough. The Columbia Pictures presidential seat he vacated was filled more recently by David Putnam, another highly ethical man whose refusal to deal in the corruption of the film business contributed to his hasty exit.

There is probably no other major business sector in America where the bumper sticker proverb--"The golden rule: them that has the gold makes the rules"-- is more in force than in Filmdom. But even if "moneyese" is the lingo of Movieland, that is one tongue we couldn't speak. We didn't have any.

We all spent days and nights praying and racking our brains, racking our brains and praying. Campus Crusade's Bill Bright was one of the more troubled. This was not a new burden for him. For years he had been seeking avenues to communicate with studio heads

115

in general and Lew Wasserman in particular to share his concern about the increasing number of movies that undermine Judeo-Christian values. This motivation had been central to his agreement to attend the screening of *Temptation.* Now Dr. Bright's concern was not general. It was all too specific. It was a deeply disturbing attack on Christ Himself.

During one of those sleepless nights Bill slipped to his knees to seek God's direction as to what to do about this hideous character assassination of his cherished Lord. It was the wee hours, and Bill's heart, broken and angry, cried out to God for an answer. The heavens were silent.

Then, as if being projected by a laser beam onto the silver screen of Bill's consciousness, came the message, "OFFER TO BUY THE FILM!" A rush of excitement flooded Bill's soul! As he often says, "Every corpuscle in my being stood on tiptoes!" This was the answer, "OFFER TO BUY THE FILM!"

Tim and I first heard of the idea from Bill's Director of Communications, Don Beehler. Sharing it in confidence with us to test the waters a bit, Don asked us what we thought of it. Almost in unison Tim and I agreed that it was genius, the kind of genius that only our God could originate. It resonated with both of us at the level of our inner man. But where would we get the money? Don said Bill felt that Christians all over the world would be willing to pitch in to protect their Lord from defamation. We agreed. How would we make it clear that neither Bill Bright, Campus Crusade, nor any other individual nor ministry would profit from the plan? We would have to have an "escrow account" into which the money would be put to guarantee its use for the intended purpose. What would we do with the film if Universal sold it to us? We would then own it. We could do with it what we wanted. We would probably have a public celebration and burn it.

I loved the idea because, for my money, it created a classic dilemma for Universal a lose/lose situation. I saw it this way:

If Universal leaders agree to sell the film:

1. They never live it down: "Universal Pictures: The only studio in town that ever knuckled under to the Christians."

2. They open themselves to criticism: "How can you take money from earnest Christians to pay for your own dumb business decision?"

3. They are admitting that the picture is a mistake: "We are selling it to cover our own wrong decision in making a film attacking Christ."

4. The movie community is on their case: "How can you sell this film for destruction? You are contributing to something akin to *censorship,* to the likes of book burning!"

5. They risk losing a possible box office bonanza that could rescue their poorly performing corporation, a box office windfall created by the controversy.

If Universal leaders do *not* agree to sell the film:

117

1. They never live it down: "Universal had a chance to sell a questionable money maker, recover its costs, and get the Christian monkey off its back, and they *didn't take it!*"

2. They open themselves for criticism: "Now it's clear that you couldn't care less about the deeply held, religious beliefs of millions. You even had a chance to recover your investment and remove the offense, and you still decided to stick it to the Christians."

3. They hold themselves up to question for past business transactions in which they have pressured other companies to sell films to them, and then have used the purchased films to further *their* own ends.

4. They appear callous in the face of a very reasonable offer: "The Christians are offering to help you get off the hook, and you won't even talk to them?"

5. They expose themselves to their stockholders: "You had a net *loss* of millions on that film at the box office! You could have cashed out 'even Steven' and have avoided the long term bad PR, if only you had taken the Christians' offer! What kind of management is that?"

The thing Tim and I liked most about the idea, in addition to the box in which it put Universal, was that it *recaptured the offensive!* We knew that from the moment the offer was released to the press every news gathering agency in America would have its representative camped on the threshhold of the Onyx Obelisk waiting for an answer. For months the gang at

118

Universal had been playing a cat and mouse game with the press, taking lots of "no comment" postures. The offer would smoke them out and force them to respond publicly.

We decided to let the entire "coalition" in on the idea to get additional wisdom and prayer support. Jack Hayford and Lloyd Ogilvie were brought on board. We weighed a lot more factors:

*   If we made the offer, we had to be prepared for it to be accepted, or it would be a sham.

*   If the offer were accepted, we had better be mighty sure we could come up with the money, or the end would be more embarassing than the beginning! Universal might try to "call our bluff."

*   We had better be ready to take flack from the Christian community as well as the general public. Many undoubtedly would not under-stand the offer or what was behind it, and we couldn't educate them before the offer or it would steal the surprise factor.

*   What would keep this offer from appearing to Christians and non-Christians alike like a "hostage ransom?" Might other film companies intentionally create anti-Christian films and take believers hostage to pay for them?

*   We had better count the cost of *which of us* is going to help Bill raise the money if the offer is accepted. It wouldn't be fair to leave Bill Bright hanging with the execution of a response

119

on behalf of all believers.

Calculating some of the downsides made us realize that we had really better know that God was leading us into this one. We discussed whose name(s) should go on the offer, if made. We discussed in what form the offer should be made. We discussed how and when the press should be brought on board. We considered this deeply and thoroughly for over a week.

I calculated that the chances of Universal's accepting the offer were about as good as a snow cone on the River Styx for the following four reasons:

1. Universal had to be all tied up in contractual obligations with Scorsese, who had raised about a third of the production money, and Cineplex Odeon, which also had put up about a third, plus other binding agreements with distribution, video-cassette, and international entities with a piece of the LTOC pie.

2. There is no way these men would let themselves appear to be weak and crumbling to the wishes of concerned Christians.

3. Pride

4. Pride

We had our confidence bolstered when a tough minded top executive in another film studio called the plan "brilliant" and was confident it would create a "no lose" situation for us. On a conference call with the members of the coalition we *all agreed* that the proposal was to be made. We all testified to having peace that it was the thing God was leading us to do. We agreed that, since God had initially given Bill Bright the idea, Bill should be the one to issue a request for a personal appointment with Lew Wasserman--no other MCA/Universal executive. The purpose of the meeting would be to present a proposal in person. If Wasserman refused to grant the appointment, then the offer would be made in writing and released to the press simultaneously with the delivery of the letter to Universal City. We agreed that the offer should have an expiration time limit on it so that Universal could not keep us dangling interminably with its answer.

I wrestled with the "hostage ransom" factor. I felt that was our area of greatest PR vulnerability. I asked myself if there were any biblical principle or rationale that might provide a basis for our action. Was this or was this not in the biblical tradition? How would we present the motivation for making the offer if called to do so on a biblical basis?

In a brainstorming session with Beehler, Penland, and Bright the answer came: "Of course it was in the biblical tradition! It was precisely the motivation of Calvary--one person offering to pay for the offenses of another!"

The strategy was set in motion. Bill Bright's office requested a private meeting with Lew Wasserman. The request was delivered in the afternoon with a deadline for response of 8:00 a.m. a few days later. Almost immediately we got word that "Mr. Wasserman was not handling this matter. Mr. Pollock was." At 7:55 a.m. on the "deadline" morning a very nervous secretary from Mr. Wasserman's office called Tim to *make sure* that he had gotten the message. We got the message all

121

right! Lew Wasserman would *not* meet with us!

Anticipating that Wasserman might not meet with us,
Don Beehler had drafted a letter to him on behalf of Bill
Bright. The epistle included substantial content from
Pope John Paul's 1987 address to the media (the
presentation which Wasserman had chaired) and input
from Tim Penland, Dr. Bright, and others:

Dear Mr. Wasserman:

I am sorry that you were unavailable for a
private meeting with our group. We
wanted to discuss a proposal with you whereby
I would personally be responsible
for reimbursing Universal Pictures for the
amount already invested in the movie
The Last Temptation of Christ. In exchange,
you would provide me with all of the
copies of the film (which would promptly be
destroyed) and its distribution rights.
I anticipate that the money will be provided by
concerned individuals across America who will
pool their resources in order to cover your
costs.

Although I do not represent any particular
religious group or denomination in this
matter, I stand in the tradition of classical
Christianity which embraces all the
major branches of Christendom.

I would like to discuss this proposal with you
in the same spirit in which Pope John
Paul II told the media in Los Angeles last
September, "The church stands ready to

122

help you by her encouragement and to support you in all your worthy aims."

The letter quoted extensively from Pope John Paul's appeal to the media community to exercise its influence responsibly and concluded:

The central message of the Christian faith is that Jesus Christ paid for our sins on the cross, and that by accepting His gift of salvation we are able to choose eternal life over death. It is in the spirit of the Savior of all men who paid for my mistakes that I am prepared to help you in this way.

Please contact my office at 714/886-5224, ext. 3100 by July 19 with your response.

Sincerely,

(Signed)

Bill Bright

cc: Pat Broeske/John Dart, the *Los Angeles Times*

The strategy worked. Did it ever work! Teams of attorneys and executives poured over the offer, analyzing it from every possible angle. Word from the inside indicated that cadres of legal beagles and frenzied managers sweated and strained over the offer's implications. More solicitors and PR men worked through a response that could be released with little risk and a plan to release it.

Meanwhile, as we predicted, the reporters descended on the U. P. castle only to find the drawbridge back in the "up" position. So, camping along the moat and lobbing messages tied to rocks over the wall, the legions of press persons awaited the response of the lords of the Universal manor. They waited. And they waited. *Five days* they waited with no response! *Five days* the turmoil inside the walls continued!

On the sixth day the royal herald strode out of the lowered bridge and carried scrolls to a handful of major newspaper offices across America--New York, Washington, Atlanta, Seattle, and Los Angeles. There he plunked down an estimated $100,000 in coinage to place full page ads.

The ads summarized Universal's view of the situation on the film, repeating the deceptive half-truth that "conservative Christian leaders" were invited to a screening which they "declined to attend." The summary highlighted the call for the *"destruction"* of the film from the July 12 press conference and the offer by Bill Bright to reimburse Universal for the cost of the film in exchange for copies *"which would promptly be destroyed."* Then they printed their open letter:

Dear Mr. Bright:

We, at Universal Pictures, have received your proposal in which you have offered to buy *The Last Temptation of Christ* which you would then destroy so that no one could ever see it. While we understand the deep feelings and convictions which have prompted this offer, we believe that to accept it would threaten the fundamental freedoms of religion and expression promised to all Americans under our Constitution.

You have quoted Pope John Paul II on the film industry's "accountability to God, to the community and before the witness of history." Those who wrote the Constitution believed that all of these were best served by protecting freedom of speech, freedom of press, and freedom of religion. As Thomas Jefferson noted, "Torrents of blood have been spilt in the old world in consequence of vain attempts . . . to extinguish religious discord by proscribing all differences of religious opinion." The Twentieth Century has provided us with further evidence of the abuses which occur when monolithic authorities regulate artistic expression and religious beliefs. Though those in power may justify the burning of books at the time, the witness of history teaches the importance of standing up for freedom of conscience even when the view being expressed may be unpopular.

You have expressed a concern that the content of the films be "true." But whose truth? If everyone in America agreed on all religious, political and artistic truths, there would be no need for our constitutional guarantees. Only in totalitarian states are all people forced to accept one version of truth. In any case, Martin Scorsese has stated clearly that his film is a work of fiction and that it is based on a novel, not the Gospels. It makes no claim whatsoever to be any more than a reflection of

125

his own personal exploration.

In your letter you state that your position "embraces all the major branches of Christendom." But there always have been and continue to be many viewpoints among Christians. Many religious leaders of different denominations who attended our July 12 screenings in New York, which you declined to attend, were not offended by the film and even felt that it could be a tool for fruitful discussion. The constitutional guarantee of freedom of religious expression was provided precisely to protect such diversity of opinions, including the highly personal views of Nikos Kazantzakis, Martin Scorsese, the film's writers and artists.

In the United States, no one sect or coalition has the power to set boundaries around each person's freedom to explore religious and philosophical questions whether through speech, books or film.

These freedoms protect all of us.

They are precious.

They are not for sale.

Universal Pictures

It was Hollywood at its best. Powerful images with little, if any, substance. As you moved through the paragraphs, you could almost see the Pilgrims persecuted by the state church in England, the Nazi

126

book burners in Germany, the Soviet states brainwashing their citizens, the Salem witch trials, and the McCarthy hearings on un-American activity. As you neared the end of the letter, you could hear *God, Bless America* coming up behind the narrator who declares for all of us at the Fourth of July rally to hear, "These freedoms protect all of us! They are precious! They are *not for sale!!*" The flag is unfurled. The crowd stands to its feet, cheering. There is a lump in every throat, a moist eye for the Republic.

Never mind that nobody called for any agency of church or state to destroy anything. We called for the alchemists who created the lethal potion to *destroy it themselves* out of respect for the well being of their fellow Americans or *sell it to us* so that it could be handled like a shipment of cocaine. Never mind that nobody called for "monolithic authorities" to "regulate artistic expression and religious belief." Such a prospect is more threatening to religion than to art!

Never mind that Scorsese's "personal exploration" and "highly personal views" describe a good man as a traitor to his own people and a liar, a pure man as a voyeur watching the first century equivalent of a porno flic in Magdalene's brothel and fornicating in his fantasies, a strong man as fainting and bedeviled--all of this *without one scintilla of historical evidence to support his "fiction."*

The heart of the letter was the question, "whose truth?" This was Hollywood's reflection of the ethos of our age in which the only absolute is that there are no absolutes. The only morality is that there is no definition of morality outside yourself. The only objective reality is that there is no objective reality

--no "fact" in history, no truth in experience, no cosmic limits on behavior. This approach was in the great tradition of a first century Roman governor who asked the same question, "What is truth?" and, not finding the truth he wanted to find, also allowed Jesus to be crucified.

So, Universal's corporate decision makers decided not to "sell America's freedoms"--which statement also reflected their arrogance--as if they *owned* America's freedoms. The offer was categorically rejected.

The anticipated backlash from Christians to the offer certainly materialized. Most of them across the nation got Universal's "answer" without getting Bill Bright's "question." Condensed in the press, the report was that Bill Bright--not Bill Bright *on behalf of the Christian community* --was offering to pay $10,000,000 for the film--not that he would *take responsibility to raise it.* Thus, there were some cries of "ransom money."

A small number of donors to Campus Crusade for Christ, perceiving that Bill Bright had offered this sum, wrote saying that "if he had that kind of money to buy off Universal, he didn't need their money." I can understand how the person in the pew, whose closest association with "big dollars" is his mortgage payment, could have a visceral reaction to *ten million dollars* for *anything*--especially if he didn't understand it and had heard only part of the story. Fortunately, most were more confused by the offer than hostile to it. But this fact didn't do much to salve those who were upset.

A few days later, Don Beehler told Tim and me that he thought Bill could use some encouragement. Bill had

128

felt, with all his heart, that he had done the right thing. It wasn't fun having a backlash like this.

I called him, the man with whom I had worked shoulder to shoulder for nearly fifteen years. "Bill," I said, "I want to encourage you. You and I have been through enough campaigns over the years to know that God is faithful, that he will reward your obedience. There is no question that God led you in this. Tim and I and the others will defend your decision to anyone. We love you." I prayed for him on the phone.

The response of the Black Tower moguls to the buyout proposal was one more indication of what seemed to be arrogant disregard for the sensitivities of Christians and disrespect for the record of history about a Man who will someday judge the living and the dead. Regardless of what anybody says, the buyout proposal worked. It forced Universal to defend the indefensible and proved that, even if we talked their language, money, they were committed to shoving this picture down our throats.

8

The Value War

The battle over *Last Temptation* is one more skirmish in the century's struggle over whose values, whose beliefs shall be exalted in American culture, and whose may be derided and disparaged.[17]

- Columnist Patrick J. Buchanan

All of life is a matter of values. At the basic level of living one must decide if the value he places on ease is going to be allowed to push out the value he places on eating. A parent must decide if unmarked walls are of higher value than his child's artistic freedom. In marriage a person must decide whether the value placed on a spouse is higher than the value placed on fleeting sexual excitement with other lovers. A pregnant mother must decide if the value of her unborn child is to be placed at a higher or lower level than her personal desires or convenience. In government the populace constantly must choose whether the value of having a powerful, centralized structure is to be valued more highly than individual autonomy.

There are probably no arenas in American life in which the shifting cultural values are in more violent conflict than in the areas of First Amendment freedoms. Does the value of a free press give Larry Flynt of *Hustler* magazine the right to publish hideous slurs against Jerry Falwell's mother? The Supreme Court seemed to think so. Does the First Amendment protect anything you choose to speak, wherever and to whomever you choose to speak it? The Supreme Court has never said it does, though this is a common perception of First Amendment protection. But even if the Supreme Court said that the Constitution protected your "right" to shout "nigger," "dago," "spic," or "wetback" at members of the human community, there would be a *higher law* in the real world that should prevent you from doing that!

The leadership of MCA/Universal must have been preoccupied on the studio lot for a couple or three decades creating mechanical King Kong's for the tour, whipping out teen sexploitation flics for the theaters, or cutting international deals for *Murder, She Wrote*. Apparently, life in the *real* world, where major problems are not solved in twenty seven minutes of air time (minus canned laughter), must have passed them by. This is the most charitable rationale I can give for their decision to underwrite Scorsese's production and then to release *The Last Temptation of Christ*.

If Universal is out of touch with the broad spectrum of American values, it is representative of the rest of media. A Connecticut Mutual Life Insurance Company study of American values compared the values of the typical American with the values of various leadership groups. The leadership group with values *most* like those of the typical American were *ministers*, followed by businessmen! The three leadership groups with values *least* like those of the typical American were, in this order, *media*, education, and science.[18] The media community is so small and so isolated from the rank and file American that it is seriously out of touch with what the rest of America is thinking. It is clear in the LTOC case that Universal thought it had a better bead on

131

American values than did the ministers! It was proved wrong.

Another graphic example of the out-of-touchness of media values with those of John and Mary Doe is the outcome of the 1984 elections. From Hollywood political fundraisers to television and radio editorials to newspaper publishers and editors--virtually all came out in favor of the Mondale-Ferraro ticket. Yet the American people gave Mondale the worst political trouncing since Alf Landon was walloped by Roosevelt in 1936!

To postulate that Universal Pictures and Cineplex Odeon were out of touch with the American people is one of the more charitable explanations as to why they underwrote, produced, released, and screened *The Last Temptation of Christ*. From the weight of evidence presented in this work alone, it is borderline lunacy to suggest that Universal big wigs released the film because they were *innocently ignorant*--that they *could not have seen nor known* the storm climate into which they were launching their craft!

Another explanation tossed around by the press and some Christians has been that "fundamentalists" (there's that word again!) were smarting from the hits they took during the televangelism scandals and were sitting on their front porch swings south of the Mason-Dixon line with their 'coon rifles loaded just *waitin' for a chance to get even*. I don't think that even *begins* to explain the breadth and depth of the national firestorm started by one low budget movie. I don't know a single Christian leader--fundamentalist or not --who hasn't been surprised by the responses and reactions of his own people to this situation . . . when

132

his people have had full information.

There are a lot of ministers, Catholic and protestant, who took a ho-hum approach to the issues raised by this film and were about run out of town by their normally apathetic laity! In describing one such situation, the editor of a Glendale, California, newspaper said, "Larry, this clearly was a case where the sheep were out ahead of the shepherds."

If you can't explain the impassioned and widespread national protest by the extremeness of the film's content, and if adding in the "televangelism backlash factor" to the equation still doesn't balance it out, what does?

I believe that Universal Pictures got caught in the middle of a *national war over values* which it didn't start and didn't finish. I feel deeply that this war has been heating up over the last two decades to the point that it was ready to break into open hostilities at any moment. To inflame things further, the opponents in the war were at distant poles of the value spectrum-- they couldn't have been farther apart! Hollywood tends to be, both morally and politically, to the left of the left. Historic Christians of all stripes tend to be the right with fundamentalists to the right of the right. Finally, both sides in the war saw the situation as a fight for the *raw survival* of their system of values --they both felt that if they lost this one, it was all over. The rush of the major studios, the writers' guild, and the directors' guild to the aid of Universal indicated that Hollywood was scared witless that they might have continuing accountability to, of all interest groups, *Christians!* Christians were scared silly that if Hollywood got away with this one, it would signal the beginning of massive persecution of them and their deeply held beliefs!

Since the sixties, when bands of student revolutionaries captured university campuses, sent money to a "democractic revolutionary" in Cuba named Fidel Castro, experimented with free sex, hard rock and LSD at Woodstock, and burned draft cards to protest the Vietnam War, there has been an assault on traditional American values from the far political and moral *left*. The elder generation, seeing its cherished halls of learning turned into armed camps, Fidel Castro turn out to be a communist dictator, their kids plagued with VD and fried brains, and respect for God and country dashed, moved aggressively to defend *its* system of values, *conservative* values. The war was on. Hollywood was and is in the middle of the war which continues to be fought on a number of battlegrounds.

Battleground Number One: Family and Marriage Values

It boggles the mind to think of it now, but thirty years or so ago it was considered a liability in Hollywood to be divorced. Elizabeth Taylor's and Zsa Zsa Gabor's "marital roulette" lifestyles were symbols of "Hollywood marriages," and, while this way of living gave them continued headlines in the gossip columns, it did not endear them to the American public. I remember a sixties comedian throwing one-liners around about Hollywood's "wash and wear wedding gowns" and the one Hollywood kid who said to the other, "Watch out, or my dad will beat up on your dad!" The other replied, "Wha-da-ya-mean? Your dad *is* my dad!"

134

In that same era a Hollywood personality who got pregnant had a secret (and expensive) abortion or went into hiding to avoid the pregnancy's being discovered in the press. Today, live-in couples are commonplace, are featured in *People* magazine without shame, and have children or abortions with little fear that it might negatively affect their careers. Fornication is so common in Hollywood and in Screenland movie and TV product that it is a subject for teenagers in sitcoms. In one study of sexual relationships depicted on television, 83% were outside the bond of marriage.[19]

In Hollywood, where top executives of all three networks have told me that homosexuals are the most powerful lobby group in the industry, a sodomy lifestyle is unbelievably common. One major production company, one major media company, and two major parts of the industry--dancing and makeup --have the reputation throughout the business of being virtually controlled by gays and lesbians.

The marriage and family battlefield can be laid out clearly by the following research on the values of the media people involved in the entertainment industry versus those of the American public:

Considered morally wrong:	Public %	Entertainment %
Abortion	65	3
Homosexuality	71	5
Adultery	85	16

Connecticut Mutual Life Report on American Values in the 80's,The Impact of Belief, pp. 201-203.

Remember, too, that this *Last Temptation* war between Hollywood values and the populace focused on the *Christians*, a group far more committed to the wrongness of the above three practices (and many other Hollywood practices) than the general public. So the disparity between the two columns above would be even greater than the figures shown!

Battlefield Number Two: Artistic Freedom

A major escalation in the war over *Temptation* occurred when the Motion Picture Association of America, the movie studios' professional organization, got into the fray. Its president, Jack Valenti, issued a statement over the names of Columbia, Disney, MGM/UA, Orion, Paramount, Fox, and Warner supporting Universal Studios in its position on LTOC. In that statement Valenti said,

> The key issue, the only issue, is whether or not self-appointed groups can prevent a film from being exhibited to the public, or a book from being published, or a piece of art from being shown . . . . The major companies of MPAA support MCA/Universal in its *absolute right to offer to the people whatever movie it chooses* [emphasis added].[20]

This statement creates a number of mysteries. Let's look at a few of them.

First of all, it's mysterious to me to hear Hollywood talking about anything "absolute." Judging from many of the films coming out of filmland, I thought the only absolute was that there were no absolutes! The sanctity of marriage isn't an *absolute*. You can portray adultery as "adult's play" in the same way you can portray children in child's play. Despite what might appear in all of nature and the animal kingdom as an *absolute*, heterosexual love, you can put people in movies and TV stories making love with the same sex, both sexes, animals or, presumably, trees. Being law abiding isn't an *absolute*. Rare is the flick that doesn't depict police, investigators, attorneys, and the common man willing to set aside obedience to law or duly constituted authority to accomplish personal ends. After so much pounding with moral notions like "if it feels good, do it," "different strokes for different folks," and "alternative lifestyles" it is a little hollow hearing Valenti proclaim a filmmaker's *absolutes*.

Then we hear Mr. Valenti, a professed Catholic Christian, articulating Universal's absolute *right* to offer to the people whatever movie it chooses. If it seems a little strange hearing him declare the film industry's "absolute right" to attack his (or anybody else's) lord in a movie offered to the public, it is *not* strange to hear him talking about rights in the context of the First Amendment or censorship. He is a spokesperson for an industry that can only thrive and survive with the guarantees of free expression afforded by the U. S. Constitution.

The mysterious thing about this is the absence of any talk about *responsibility*. If I were to make a ten million dollar movie depicting Mr. Valenti's mother as an emotionally disturbed child molester, I wonder if he would be on the stump across America proclaiming my "absolute right" to release it and declaring that his only response would be, "I just won't pay six bucks to see it!" I have a hunch such a situation would call up some other moral or even *Christian* principle in Mr.

137

Valenti, like, perhaps, the Golden Rule. But, then, the movie industry signs his paycheck.

The final mystery to me is how this specific situation with Univeral Pictures fits with past ones. Thomas Pryor, writing in *Variety*, called this protest "the ultimate expression of censorship," based on a situation in which he was involved years ago.[21] I wonder if *any* previous situation fits this one. Pryor, unlike Valenti, recognizes that there are limits on First Amendment freedoms. He quotes the often repeated example that the first amendment does not give a person the right to shout "fire" in a crowded theater, presumably because of resulting injury.

There are several, major differences between the flap over *The Last Temptation of Christ* and previous Hollywood scrapes with the public. If Universal Pictures represents the person whose freedom to cry "fire" is limited by the Frst Amendment, then consider the following. First, Universal gave thorough, advance consideration as to what it might yell in its theaters. It hired consultants to give it counsel on what it might scream and how its shouts might be received. Doing our jobs as consultants, Tim Penland warned Universal repeatedly in person, and I warned them in my research paper on Christians that "shouting" this film in theaters would bring immense wrath down on them.

Secondly, this shout was *scripted*. Once the public had knowledge of the contents of two versions of the script, there was little ambiguity as to what Tom Pollock and Martin Scorscese were intending to shout and that it would be considered injurious by a significant segment the populace. The twenty plus years of angry Christian reaction to the novel on which the film was based

138

should have given them that message. People in theaters seldom get advance warning as to what other theatergoers intend to shout. This time the people got to see an *advance script* of it! Needless to say, much of the American public was furious to discover that it was the object of *premeditated* injury.

Finally, Universal's announced determination to shout "fire" with this film in theaters--*despite* the pleas of those standing to be injured by it, *despite* the business and financial disaster it brought upon itself, and *despite* the decades of ill will it brought to its corporate image and the image of the other, responsible movie makers in Hollywood--is incredible! Now that they've screamed this message of a profaned Christ and of contempt for Christian sentiment in many theaters, they may well deserve being trampled to death in the stampede that follows. Be assured of this: the First Amendment won't be able to resurrect them. Perhaps Universal Pictures needs to recall that the First Amendment wasn't handed down by God, but the first *commandment* --against having other Gods--*was!*

Battlefield Number Three: Religious Faith

When Ben Stein wrote his insightful classic on the values of Hollywood, *The View From Sunset Boulevard,* He covered Hollywood's view of everything from big business to small towns, from the police to the poor, from crime to the clergy. In his chapter on ministers and religion Stein noted that ministers and faith are *irrelevant* to Hollywood.

I cannot remember any recent episode in which a character was moved by religious feelings to do or not to do any important act.

In short, religion is something about which little interest is shown on prime time television . . . The views of TV writers and producers toward organized religion are extremely consistent with the depiction of religion as an irrelevancy. Most of those interviewed did not see religion as a significant fact *in their lives or in the national life* [emphasis added]. [22]

Ben Stein said that the comments of Lee Rich, past president of Lorimar and MGM/UA and one involved in creating such shows as *Eight is Enough, The Waltons,* and *thirtysomething,* tended to embrace the comments of many others interviewed:

Is the church important in American life? No. . . . The church has destroyed itself over a number of years . . . . I gave up the church at 17. I don't know anyone who goes to church . . . . The church has been narrow minded. It hasn't grown up with the times. [23]

One woman producer, who did not want her name used in Stein's research, saw religion as a "fundamental non-issue in American life" except in an area in which she had strong feelings, her support for abortion, where she saw organized religion as "highly negative."

As mentioned earlier, the Connecticut Mutual Life Report on American Values indicated that people in media seldom or never prayed, read sacred scriptures, or participated in religious activities. 93% *seldom* or *never* attend a religious observance of *any kind!* [24]

The above generalizations disguise a significant and

140

rapidly growing Christian presence among professionals in film and television. After nine years of
working with this segment of Hollywood, I can say that
finally believers are coming out of the woodwork and
are beginning, very tentatively, to admit they are both
deeply religious and Christian in an environment which
is hostile or apathetic to both.

In this presentation of the "religious factor" in the
LTOC acrimony, I dare not ignore a hideous distortion of
the outcry against *The Last Temptation* which
attempted to place the reponsibility for this film at the
feet of *Jews*. Nearly every time Rev. R. L. Hymers,
Jr., spoke he was saying something like "Jewish money
is bankrolling this anti-Christian film." That isn't a
new suggestion, i.e. that the reason that Hollywood is so
rotten or anti-Christian is that it is so *Jewish*.

Jewish it is. Though 45% of the media elite presently
claim no religious affiliation, 59% of media leadership
in general reported Jewish upbringings.[25] And my
observation is that the higher you go in the power
structure of film and television, the more Jewish the
industry becomes. If you don't believe me, check out
the corporate directors of the ten biggest movie studios
sometime.

But the problem isn't that the media elite is Jewish.
The problem is that it isn't Jewish *enough!* In like
manner, the problem isn't that there are Catholics and
protestants in media, the problem is that they aren't
enough Catholic or protestant! The point is that media
leaders of all persuasions have forsaken or have never
acquired the moral and ethical values and spiritual
commitments of their religious roots. On the other side

of this battlefield from Universal were legions of Catholics, protestants, orthodox, and even Jews and a few Muslims. But the thing that put them on the opposite side of the field from the Moguls of Tinseltown was that they were *very deeply religious.*

Temptation is a wonderful case in point. The novel was written by a man, Nikos Kazantzakis, whose intense exposure to Christianity was six months in a monastic cell on Mt. Athos which he left when he failed to find God and conquer his passions. He then became a disciple of Nietsche, Lenin, and Buddha before writing his controversial novel. After dabbling in these divergent philosophies, he never became a religious devotee´ of Christ or Buddha or any religion. While Kazantzakis gave lipservice to Christ, P. A. Bien, the biographer who summed up Kazantzakis' life in many editions of the book, *The Last Temptation of Christ,* said:

> Since, for Kazantzakis, freedom is not a reward for the struggle but rather the very process of the struggle itself, it is paramount that Jesus be constantly tempted by evil in such a way that he feel its attractiveness and even succumb to it, for only in this way can his ultimate rejection of temptation have meaning.
>
> *This is heresy* . . . The fact that Kazantzakis not only slipped into this heresy but *deliberately made it the keystone of his structure* should give us some clue to his deepest aims. He was not primarily interested in reinterpreting Christ or in disagreeing with, or reforming the Church. He wanted, rather, to lift Christ out of the Church altogether and . . . to rise to the occasion and

exercise man's right (and duty) to *fashion a new saviour* and thereby *rescue himself from a moral and spiritual void.* [emphasis added].[26]

Kazantzakis' tombstone bore an inscription of his own creation which expressed, in its own way, a commitment to non-religion "I have nothing . . . I fear nothing . . . I am free."[27]

Martin Scorsese is a man who, by his own admission, is not a "practicing" Catholic, though he does claim to be a "Catholic." He was kicked out of a junior seminary at 14 and became alienated from the Roman Catholic Church in the early seventies. It would not appear that he has ever committed himself to the Christ of his religious roots, as evidenced by the Christ to which he was first attracted years ago in the Kazantzakis novel, the Christ he distorted far more radically in his own film. While Scorsese claims to be a Christian, it is hard to see how his ethics, his lifestyle, and his cinematic creations are at all compatible with the values of Christ or Roman Catholic Christianity.

Paul Schrader is a protestant who also does not appear to practice the faith of his upbringing in the Dutch Reformed Church. Schrader does not practice the teachings of the protestant Christian faith or create films from a Christian world view. A number of acquaintances who were at Calvin College where he was graduated told me of the heartbreak he has caused those close to him by his departure from his childhood faith.

Lew Wasserman, Sid Sheinberg, and Tom Pollock are three Jews in the LTOC mix. A quick check with their

143

rabbis would indicate whether or not they could be more faithful to Judaism. Judging from our dealings with them, they could be considerably more committed to the ethical and moral values of the Torah.

All of this is *not* to say that the major leadership of the protest against *Temptation* walk on water. We clearly do not. It *is* to say that the battlefield was divided on the basis, not of Jew against Christian or Christian against Jew, but *deeply religious* against *hardly religious* or *not religious at all*.

And here is the ultimate zinger! In the issues surrounding *The Last Temptation of Christ* the war was fought on *all of the above battlefields at the same time!* This film packaged into one, two hour and forty minute parcel the following moral issues that the folks at the religious end of the faith continuum found offensive:

Complicity	*Jesus fashioning crosses used by Romans to kill Jews*
Pornography	*Jesus watching Magdalene have sex and having sex on screen*
Immodesty	*Full female frontal nudity at the baptism of Jesus*
Violence	*Bloody animal sacrifices and graphic crucifixion scenes*
Gore	*Jesus pulling his bloody heart out of his body*
Sacrilege	*Jesus eating a bloody apple offered to him by Satan*
Bigamy or	*Jesus marrying both Mary and Martha of Bethany*
Adultery	*Jesus committing adultery with Martha of Bethany*
Fornication	*Magdalene shown fornicating*

	with eight to ten men
Blasphemy	*Jesus confessing His need for purification*
Disrespect	*Attacking the character of a cherished leader*
Irreverence	*Holding deity or sacred things up to ridicule*
Profanity	*Treating sacred things in a common manner*

Were the above offenses *in the film* not sufficient to stir the ire of the deeply religious and generally decent American, the following were cherished values violated *by the studio:*

Discrimination	*Releasing a film a religious group finds offensive*
Lying	*Altering a historical record disguised as "fiction"*
Irresponsibility	*Producing/releasing a film without moral restraint*
Callousness	*Refusing even to hear the pleas of millions*
Greed	*Seeking to profit from offenses against others*
Abuse of tradition	*Taking Constitutional freedoms beyond reason*
Breaking film ethics	*Fictionalizing history without fictional names*
Arrogance	*Flying in the face of reasonable requests for relief*
Unreasonableness	*Refusing an offer to reimburse their investment*
Duplicity	*Deceiving Christian leaders and consultants*

Every one of the values in the left hand column is strongly condemned by those whose values are part of the American, Judeo-Christian system. Each of those is strongly denounced as *sin* by the Christian community.

Any wonder why there was a national outcry over this film?

To all of this, the Warren Beatty's, Sidney Pollack's, and Norman Lear's of the show biz world bemoaned the inevitable "chilling effect" this protest might have on "artistic freedom." This same argument is used as camouflage by pornography kings.

My response? Successful living is a matter of living within moral limits. If there were no "chilling effect" from black and white cars, speeding tickets, and judges in black robes with the power to separate you from your hard earned money or your freedom to roam freely in society, how much more chaos and bloodshed would we have on the highways? If there were no "chilling effect" of having your spouse find out that you have a secret lover, how much more infidelity would there be in marriage? It is the fact that there is "hell to pay" in the life hereafter that provides enough of a "chilling effect" to keep the human race from creating more of a hell here. If there is no "chilling effect" for film and TV producers from the deeply religious *majority* in America, we will be seeing child molesting, cannibalism, sado-masochism, bestiality, and "snuff" films soon accepted as "art" on the major movie screens of America. If that sounds ludicrous to you, remember that *the things films are now showing* would have sounded ludicrous to predict only three or four decades ago!

146

This is precisely why millions of Americans hit the fan over *Last Temptation.* It symbolized for them the crossing of a major, new threshold--not of art or creativity--but of cinematic license. When that license was taken with the Person who is responsible for providing forgiveness, hope, peace, healing, power, and eternal life for 185 million Americans, those most committed to the biblical/historical Christ shouted . . .

"Enough, already! Bring on the chilling effect! To lose the war over my personal God and Savior is to lose life itself!"

9

The Demolition Crew

It had been a while since I had seen my good friend, Jay Rodriguez. I sat across the desk from him in his tidy and tastefully decorated office at NBC in Burbank as we tried to catch up on what had been happening in each other's lives. Jay is NBC vice president for public relations, west coast, a veteran PR man in the entertainment business, and the quality of guy that collects only friends, not enemies. I had briefed Jay on the events of my life since we had last seen each other, and he was having his turn.

It was shortly after the U. S. armed military action in Grenada (I guess President Reagan never called it an "invasion"), and Jay was commenting on a stunning phenomenon the PR department at NBC had just experienced.

"Larry, we had something happen that was really surprising to us. The other evening on the network news, John Chancellor gave a very restrained editorial about the Grenada situation. He noted with some concern that the media were excluded completely from the operation. The press was not informed of the action beforehand and was not included as part of the military contingent that went into Grenada. He observed that this action violated a tradition of press coverage of U. S. military operations, and expressed his concern that this decision could set a dangerous precedent."

"We were *flooded* with calls and letters regarding what we thought was a very moderate and restrained editorial. We received thousands of responses, which was surprising enough. But the responses were running more than 90% *in favor* of President Reagan's *exclusion* of the press! That was a real shock. Larry, we don't get 90% response from viewers in support of *motherhood!*"

We chatted a bit about the implications of that experience and agreed that there seems to be a significant and growing *suspicion of* or *contempt for* the American press corps. After being personally involved in two situations that were covered by the national press prior to the LT flap, I can begin to understand why. It can be an extremely frustrating and disillusioning experience. Discovering how the press operates is a little like discovering how American democracy *really* works after you have had your image of our government shaped by a high school civics course! If you love sausage, respect laws, and trust news stories, I hope you never find out how any of them is made!

The more we worked with the press, the more we appreciated the "miracle" we felt God worked in giving us such great coverage from the initial press conference held on July 12. That conference, which was a major factor in launching the protest on the West Coast, was covered very accurately and fairly by both the print and electronic media. We don't know of a *single story* coming out of that conference that was skewed against us. Even the entertainment trade publications covered the story with balance and objectivity usually reserved for one of their own.

But it didn't last long. Within a few days the press had reverted to a previous evolutionary state and was operating with its inherent Neanderthal filters, biases, prejudices, and distortion techniques intact. Beyond that first week it became almost impossible for us to get our side of the story told. We couldn't get anything approaching objective journalistic treatment, or even balanced coverage of our cause.

I am aware that some fine journalists in both print and electronic media and some responsible members of the press who have become respected friends may get painted with the brush I use here. If that happens, it will be most unfortunate. I will have unintentionally used some of the same techniques that I will be decrying. So, please note that I will be describing a *majority* of those press people and structures with which we have had to deal. Do not apply the generalizations I make to the *responsible* professionals who work hard to present issues thoroughly and fairly. These are the protectors of the American free press system. My concern is directed to those members of the media who pursue their own agendas at the expense of those with differing world views and even at the expense of truth.

In all fairness, I realize that the *Temptation* kind of story is much more difficult for the American media crew to cover than its usual fare. Because journalists tend to be both skeptical and irreligious, they generally don't have the foggiest idea where to begin in understanding, translating, and communicating the subtleties of a religious story. Ask any newspaper editor, and he will tell you that many reporters view the religion assignment for the paper as being only slightly better than assignment to a Siberian slave

150

labor camp. It's met with about as much enthusiasm as a teacher feels when assigned to three sections of English with eighth grade boys.

Not only is a religious story an unpopular assignment for the typical reporter, *understanding* one is like my efforts to understand my first polo game a few months ago. I didn't know a "chukker" from a "twenty goal tournament." I couldn't figure out why the scoreboard didn't start at zero for both teams, or what mysterious "line" the players were crossing when they were penalized for "crossing the line." In like manner, when even an experienced reporter covers a Christian story, he commonly can't tell you the difference between a Southern Baptist and an American one, a calvinist from a charismatic, or a fundamentalist from an adventist.

One of the most flagrant examples of the media's ignorance of Christianity was when Los Angeles CBS entertainment reporter, Steve Kmetko, wrapped up his review of *The Last Temptation* by stating authoritatively, "As far as the controversy goes, the movie *follows Christian doctrine very closely*." I have no idea what seminary gave Kmetko his knowledge of Christian doctrine or what Christian church he has been attending. With a statement like that, though, I can only suspect that he was graduated from "Universal Theological Seminary" and attends the "First Unorthodox Church of Scorsese."

There is an unsilent majority in the American press corps which majors in distortion. Just a few days before I wrote this chapter, Tim called me and read a quotation from the press that was attributed to Billy Graham. The quote was represented to be taken from Dr. Graham's participation on the Larry King show as

151

the two discussed *The Last Temptation of Christ.* It was recorded in *USA Today,* Monday, August 29, 1988.

> The Rev. Billy Graham is opposed to any boycott of *The Last Temptation of Christ.* 'I fully believe in the separation of church and state, and I totally believe in the First Amendment.' Billy added that he intended to see the film, because he couldn't judge it without seeing it, and added how he couldn't understand how anyone could prejudge anything.

Tim was visibly shaken as he walked into my home for a family dinner, having just gotten hold of the statement. "Larry, I can't believe that Billy Graham is taking this position," he said. "This is going to be used against us in unbelievable ways. I am sure Billy is going to hear from a lot of his friends who are stunned that he is taking this position against them."

After reflecting Tim's concern for what I felt was a sufficient time to make sure Tim knew I wasn't taking it lightly, I laughed openly. "Tim, I can't believe Billy Graham made that statement! I know him too well to believe that he put those ingredients together in one statement or took that position at all. The reason he didn't come out more directly on this earlier was because he doesn't like to get involved in controversy. Besides, that last line really isn't his thinking. He's too smart and has been burned by the press too many times to have made a sweeping generalization like that." As we talked it through, we agreed that there was something flaky about the story which could be determined only by a call to the Billy Graham Association.

Tim called Dr. Graham's office the next morning to confirm or deny the content of the story. His office issued a statement indicating what Billy's position really was:

> Following several newspaper articles regarding his position on *The Last Temptation of Christ*, Evangelist Billy Graham issued a statement from his home in western North Carolina, saying "I do not plan to see the film, but will not take overt boycott action by demonstrating in front of a theater that may be showing it. I don't have to see a rape in order to condemn rape," Mr. Graham said. "I don't have to see a murder to condemn murder. From what I have read, this film is sacreligious.[28]

Some member of the media demolition crew had heard Billy Graham make a number of statements through his or her own system of filters, had taken them out of the larger contexts in which they were said, and had strung them together into one "statement." In so doing, he or she had demolished the integrity of many of the statements, the contexts necessary for their interpretation, the overall intent and position of Dr. Graham, and, in short, the *truth!*

In the months that we have been involved in this situation, we have seen the media go through a whole warehouse of demolition tools and use them with great effectiveness to batter many of the facts which support our position. Some of the hits we have taken have been unintentional, but many have clearly been premeditated. Let me illustrate what happens.

Demolition by Oversimplification

Temptation was not a simple news story. The story was not simply "*Christians fight film.*" Not all of the people fighting the film were Christians. Not all the people who called themselves "Christians" were fighting the film. The fighting really wasn't "fighting" in the literal sense. The fighting was taking place in a number of different arenas at a number of different levels. It was not just the film that was being fought.

In chapter eight I presented you with fourteen offensive items in the film itself. I could have given you fourteen more! This story dealt with *very* complex issues-- the historicity of Jesus Christ, the accuracy of the biblical account, the definition of censorship, the definition of blasphemy, the proper way to fictionalize historical figures, First Amendment protection and abuse, religious discrimination, and movie-making tradition.

Let's face it. This story did not lend itself to being jammed into a three to five minute slot on the six o'clock news. But, Americans usually can't be made to sit still for more than thirty minutes of news from the *whole world*. They won't sit still at all if the news isn't "entertaining" and fast moving (they've been weaned on squealing tires, sex, and violence), and they certainly are going to be bored out of their gourds if you try to cover fourteen major objections. What's a newsperson to do? Demolish it! Simplify it. Knock enough off the story so that it *will* fit into the allocated time slot, regardless of the violence it does to one or both sides.

The print media could do a better job of covering the

story, because they could devote more time and space to it. But that was little help since most Americans now get their news via TV. Then, too, the wire services, which feed most of the nation's newspapers and broadcast stations, demolished it through abbreviation so it could easily be extracted from the other end of the wire.

Once demolished, the story was not recognizable to us. The media said that the protest was by Christians (95% true), by fundamentalist Christians (75% false, depending on your definition), who objected to *one scene* in which Jesus comes down off the cross to have sex with Mary Magdalene (95% false).

Probably the worst destruction by oversimplification we witnessed was on CBS news in Los Angeles. After movie critic, Steve Kmetko, gave his review of *The Last Temptation*, the other two anchors engaged in brief repartee with Kmetko regarding the sex scene between Jesus and Magdalene.

Anchor #1: "So you mean, Steve, that all of this protest about the film surrounds the equivalent of one page from a two hundred fifty page book?"

Anchor #2: "Or really just 30 seconds of a two hour and forty minute movie?"

Kmetko: "That's it."

Next story. This treatment was so oversimplified as to be a *lie* . . . but it fit the time slot.

Demolition by Choice of Words

S. I. Hayakawa, the noted semanticist, writing in his classic work, *Language in Thought and Action*,[29] observes that in reporting something it is possible to use "snarl" words or "purr" words. When such words are used, the communicator is doing much more than reporting. He is making "direct expressions of approval or disapproval, judgments in their simplest form." A purr word statement, "She is the sweetest girl in all the world," really is not reporting. It is making a judgment, a positive one. "He's nothing but filthy scum!" a snarl word statement, is not reporting, either. It is making a negative judgment.[30] Semanticists also describe the "emotional charging" of words in a negative or positive direction.

Snarl words, purr words, and words charged in a negative direction were commonly used by the media as wrecking balls to batter our position. Without exploring or communicating our position or the thinking behind it, a number of media spokespersons used snarl words and negatively charged words to judge us. A *Variety* columnist referred to the protest as the "ultimate expression of censorship."[31] He continued, "Why attempt to enforce pre-censorship, which is basically alien to the American way of life?" In a letter to the editor of that same publication, the writer declared, "The proposed boycott of MCA and Universal Studios by right-winged Christian reactionary groups over the upcoming release of *The Last Temptation of Christ* includes a dangerous precedent: industry insiders abdicating free speech."[32]

The choice of words in just *three sentences* taken from the millions of sentences written across America about

156

this matter makes my point. We heard "ultimate . . . censorship," "precensorship," "alien," "alien to the American way of life," "boycott," "right-winged," "reactionary," "dangerous precedent," "abdicating," and "abdicating free speech." Did you learn anything about what we were saying, get any information about the content of the movie or any clarification as to what we were asking Universal (or *anybody*, for that matter) to do? No. But after all of those snarl words, it shouldn't matter. You have learned that we are extreme, disgusting, and un-American. Our position has been demolished without any reporting of the facts. The truth falls to impassioned, emotion-laden rhetoric --the wrecking ball of word choices.

Demolition by Selective Omission

I have done enough marriage counseling to understand quite well the concept of selective omission. One spouse comes in to talk with me and states what a beast her husband is, how he is physically abusive, out of control, insensitive, and justly deserving of being divorced. I discover when the husband comes in that on only one occasion, after an extensive, heated argument, the wife taunted him viciously to which he responded by giving her a shove. On one occasion a husband described how stubborn, uncooperative, prudish, nagging, critical, and unfeminine his wife was. When the wife came to see me, I was stunned at what an attractive, apparently pleasant lady she was. From his description, I fully expected to see some creature that was a combination of Vampira and a gargoyle. In reflecting back on both cases, I realized that the content of the statements by the two was largely true. The two had merely selected the worst traits of the other for disclosure, selectively omitting their positive traits or

157

parts of the story that favored the other. They used the "convenient oversight" of important parts of the story as a crowbar to pry the story their direction.

This happened commonly in the press coverage of the *Temptation* issue. Despite strong and repeated statements to the press that (1) we denounced censorship, (2) that censorship was a greater threat to religion than to art, and (3) that we recognized Universal's First Amendment freedom to produce and release films of its choosing, I challenge you to find *any thread of this thinking whatever* in the stories covering this struggle. I can remember only one story that made reference to our anti-censorship position. It resembled the following statement: "Although the critics of the film say that they are against censorship, it is clear that they are calling for just that. They are obviously more media wise that some others who, in the past, have called for the burning of books and films."

Despite the fact that, at one point *before* the theater release of the film, we had seen *two* versions of the script, had reports of *three* eyewitnesses to the film --one inside Universal and two outside--and had copious, *scene-by-scene notes* from the New York screening, this was never mentioned by the press. I challenge you to find a news account in the secular media which listed the full, documentary basis on which we were making our protest! We know of only one. And this despite the fact that we put it in writing to the press in one release. ABC's *Nightline* crew showed the Fact Sheet and quoted portions from it that fit their purposes, but they ignored the documentary basis for our position! It might be instructive to match the number of articles that ignored the bases for the protest with the hundreds of reports that said, ". . . protesting a film they *haven't seen*."

Despite the fact that we listed *eight to ten major depictions* in the film that were offensive to us as Christians on our nationally distributed Fact Sheets (like the one *Nightline* displayed), the press would not even include such critically important information-- the content of the film which we found offensive. I challenge you to find a story in the secular press reporting our position that carried more than three of our concerns. Again, we know of only one, *Time*, August 15. And, despite the fact that eyewitness accounts vindicated more than 90% of our claims regarding the content, have you heard one media person say anything like, "We gave those Christians a hard time for protesting a film they hadn't seen, but, you know, *they were right!* With minor exceptions the stuff they said was in the film *was* in there!"

You also will not find one thorough presentation of the way Universal mishandled the Christian leaders. How much have you read about the doubletalk they laid on responsible Christian leadership in a calculated plan to disarm them? Have you read even one line attacking Universal's exploitation of well intentioned and honorable ministers? What has the press told you about the secret screenings and the denials of those screenings at a time when Pollock and Company were telling Christians the film "wasn't ready" to be shown? Reporters simply would not report these things!

But "State Exhibit A" on this point is the media's continuing omission of reports on the massive quantities of mail and phone calls Universal received and is still receiving.

"State Exhibit B" is the press corp's account as to how the film ultimately did at the box office. If you are like 90% or more of America, you probably believe the press accounts that the controversy ironically turned what might have been a box office dud into a big money maker. You no doubt have seen repeated press accounts such as "sellout crowds greet opening of *Last Temptation* in ____(fill in the blank)____." You may even have seen accounts describing how the protests "backfired" causing more people to see the film than otherwise would have. Is this what you have heard?

Let me give you some facts. When this book went to press, the film had been in release for over eight weeks and had been shown on hundreds of screens both nationally and internationally. Data from the box office records in *Variety* and from two insiders in the business, one at Universal, indicated that the film had grossed only about 6.6 million dollars! It was doing so poorly that *Variety* no longer was listing its figures.

Now let me give you some educated guesses. Despite a promotion campaign which put *an additional 6 million* into advertising, the film was dead at the box office and had little chance of reaching 8 million dollars in gross theater income. Of this possible 8 million Universal's share would be approximately 3.5 million. This means that with 11 to 12 million dollars in the project by the first week of release swelled by 6 million of additional promotional dollars to 17 to 18 million dollars in costs, Universal stood to eat its shirt for as much as 9 to 10 million dollars! Even if you factor in some "miracle" revenues from videocassettes, foreign release, or television, the Big U. is going to have to explain to its stockholders the idiotic decision to alienate millions in bad corporate PR in exchange for a multi-million dollar deficit!

One possible construction to all this is that the protest and boycott of the film was *overwhelmingly successful!* What other low budget film with an estimated 10 to 20 million in free (protest) advertising and 6 to 8 million in paid advertising wouldn't even make back its paid advertising money? The boycott must have *kept away* millions even if it did send the curious to the theaters.

But have you heard this anywhere in the press? I doubt it. Even the movie trade papers have been short on any comment indicating that, even without factoring in decades of costly ill will, LTOC is a *colossal bust!*

That crowbar of selective omission has pryed, twisted, and leveraged the content of our position time and time again, wrecking it beyond recognition.

Demolition by Choice of Witnesses

If you are going to present a case with two opposing sides in your medium, be it radio, TV, video, or print media, it would seem the essence of fair play that you match the opponents. Even as you would not put the heavyweight champion of the world in the ring with the bantamweight champ, you would not do the equivalent in your media coverage of a key issue. Or would you?

Frequently we received frantic calls from radio and TV stations scrambling to get *somebody, anybody* for the program within twenty four hours of air time or less --even broadly viewed programs like Larry King, Oprah Winfrey, Morton Downey, Jr., CBS evening news with Dan Rather, or evening news on all three L. A.

networks. While some fine spokespersons for our cause were utilized, we watched program producers fill the spots at the last minute, sometimes with warm bodies.

Often the opponent would be some "official" representative of the film industry like Jack Valenti or Martin Scorsese himself. Frequently "our side" was represented by a volunteer from the Christian community who had only the remotest association with the Hollywood/Universal situation, or a person with some knowledge of the situation but with mediocre ability to articulate his knowledge in the world of big time media. The mismatchings in some cases were ludicrous. That did not seem to matter to most show producers. They appeared more interested in theater than in fair play. (I would give you some specific examples if I did not feel that to do so would reflect negatively on some fine spokespersons for our cause.)

Regardless of the merits of a position, if defended by a weak spokesperson, the position collapses. Smaaaaaaaaaaaaaash! The demolition continued.

Demolition by Stereotyping

Whether conservative Christians like it or not, they are stereotyped. The blacks have rather successfully pressured media to cast off the Amos and Andy and Aunt Jemimah stereotypes of their culture. *The Cosby Show* certainly hasn't hurt this effort. Women are making significant progress in shaking off the dumb blonde or weakling housewife image through programs like *Cagney and Lacy, L. A. Law,* and other hit shows. But Christians have failed miserably in shaking off their stereotypes. The media consistently perpetuate them.

162

Say "conservative Christian male" to the typical media person and he comes back with the following word associations: "fundamentalist-sweating-yelling-Bible thumping-narrow minded-polyester suited-white shoed-poorly educated-sexually hung up-southern accented and bigoted." Hit the female part of the equation and you get: "frilly dressed-rhinestone bedecked- bouffant hairdoed-heavily made up-sweet talking-emotionally dependent-mother of five-cries a lot-and says 'Jeeeeesuuuuuus.'" If you don't believe Christians are stereotyped, you haven't seen *Saturday Night Live's* "Church Lady!" Since the stereotype is particulary negative in many parts of the nation, you can discredit a Christian cause just by putting on your program spokespersons who fit the stereotype. Do that and even the other Christians are embarrassed to be identified with the cause.

A prime example of that was--you guessed it--Rev. R. L. Hymers, Jr. The media put him on an incredible number of shows, and he apparently was eager to be on most of them. God love him, he was embarassing the cause so badly that one show business executive who had signed the ad in *The Hollywood Reporter* called us and told us we could not use his name any more. He didn't want to be identified in any way with a cause for which Hymers was a spokesman! Tim and I both turned down Fox network's *Late Show* with Ross Shafer only to discover that brother Hymers had filled the slot. When R. L. ranted, raved, abused the host, refused to allow the other guest to speak, and then stormed off the show, I died inside.

The old Caterpillar tractor pushed one more side of our structure in. The demolition of our cause by stereoptying was a success.

163

Demolition by Association

One of the most powerful propaganda techniques is the power of association. You want your cause to have an immediate "good feel?" Use red, white, and blue and associate it with motherhood, apple pie, Uncle Sam, Mickey Mouse, and celebrities that wear white hats. Why do you think Norman Lear named his left wing media clone of the ACLU "People for *the American Way?*" Now, you tell me, how in the world could anything nefarious come from people who represent *the American way* of thinking and doing things?

In case you missed it, I used the association technique in describing Lear's organization. I called it a "clone of the ACLU." In so doing, I associated it with one of the most left-leaning, Christian-baiting structures in America. I associated it *fairly*, though, because it cooperates with and is formally associated with the ACLU in a host of efforts nationwide. PFTAW and the ACLU work together on everything from support for Universal's production and release of LTOC to the war to provide legal sanctuary for pornography kings. It would have been *unfair* association if I had linked People for the American Way with the Communist Party U.S.A., despite some obvious similarities in politics, philosophy, and world view.

One of the most unbelievable situations Tim and I got into was with the TV program that highlights show biz, *Entertainment Tonight.* We felt that *E. T.* gave us a pretty fair shake after the initial press conference, so we agreed to grant a long video interview for a special program they were doing on the implications of *Temptation.* We were assured by the representatives of the show that they wanted our side of the issues along

164

with the others. In more than an hour of videotaping, Tim and I were given the chance to share our views, defend our positions, explain our rationale, and generally "say our piece." We ended the taping with a good feeling that we had been heard. The interviewer even asked if there was anything else we wanted to say before the crew packed up the camera gear. When we said, "Yes," they rolled the cameras a bit more.

We watched with eagerness the following Monday night as the program began to unfurl across the screen. As it rolled, we were furious. The theme of the program was "censorship." Of the more than an hour of content they taped, they included only four short statements from the two of us totalling no more than 90 seconds! Not one of the statements they used was at the heart of our position, and, worst of all, they set up the piece by showing *Nazi book burning* and *South African Police confiscating film prints!* Immediately following these two scenes, *E. T.* showed the Christian march and rally at Universal Studios with the narration, "Christians move against *The Last Temptation of Christ*. Another face of censorship?"

What associations! The demolition crew had struck again, torching our structure with flames from the bonfires of Nazi book burners and South African police!

Demolition by Falsification

The final implement of demolition used on us was direct falsification. In case that big word misses the point, the press often told outright *lies* about us and our position. In fairness, most of the lies were not of the journalists' own invention. Most were "lying by omission" in which a false impression is given by

165

failing to report key ingredients of the story, or they were lies told to them by others which were repeated without checking. This is a tricky one for the press. By this definition, I told a "lie" about Tom Pollock. I attributed a statement to him which I later found out he had not said. It was not wrong intent, but it was sloppy journalism. It's going to happen in reporting--even in the content of this book--despite the best efforts of the most ethical journalist (and our best efforts in this book) to keep it from happening.

Sloppy reporting, passing on what the reporter *wanted* to believe without putting it to the test, and highlighting false statements by others were also frequent sources of falsehoods in the media. It did not help that Universal employees repeatedly gave information to the media that was false. They told the media, for example, that Tim had possessed a copy of the script for weeks, that he had seen it before he signed on with them, that nobody inside Universal had seen the film (when eyewitnesses inside had confirmed the screenings), that nobody had said, "The Christians aren't going to stop us from releasing this film!" when we had a witness to the statement, and that Universal "had no anti-Christian bias."

One good example of the dissemination of deliberate falsehoods was an interview on Channel 13 in Los Angeles. Larry Attebery interviewed Glen Gumpel, the Executive Director of the Director's Guild, just after a number of prominent Hollywood directors held a press conference supporting Universal and denouncing the protest.

Attebery: "How do you feel about the groups that are

advocating that they buy the film or take the film somehow and destroy it?"

Gumpel: "The guild and I believe they certainly have the right to protest. It is the manner in which they are protesting. They are being extremely intimidating, threatening. They threatened to slash screens. They threatened to throw paint at theaters. So we're concerned with the manner in which they are protesting, not the fact that they are."

At that point in the progression of the protest a very broad range of people--from Donald Wildmon to Mother Teresa and from Bill Bright to some Jewish rabbis--had come into the public eye objecting to the film, asking Universal not to release it, or calling for a boycott of Universal. *Not one spokesperson* had advocated that protesters ". . . take the film somehow and destroy it." The only context in which protesters discussed the destruction of the film was if it were their private property through outright purchase. To this day I have heard no movement leader advocate the *seizing* of the film.

Furthermore, *not one spokesperson* to this day has advocated the destruction of the property of others, physical violence, the slashing of screens, or the throwing of paint. The closest anyone came to this was Rev. R. L. Hymners, Jr., who dramatized in one of his street theater demonstrations what he projected, I think unwisely, people *would do* if the film were released. In that demonstration he slashed a screen and sprayed paint on it, so it was easy to see how a viewer might take that as a *veiled* threat. But for a responsible member of the film community to paint the protest by thousands of religious leaders as "threatening" and "intimidating," to use Hymers as the spokesperson for the entire protest, and to twist even what Hymers had advocated into a falsehood, was the kind of nuclear blast that the media demolition crew used to atomize the position of the Christian community.

Another stunning evidence of falsifying was revealed on a radio talk show in which I participated on a Seattle station. A guest on the program was Michael Medved of *Sneak Previews* who hated the film as a movie critic. When asked if the film was so bad why did so many critics come out in favor of it, he stated that he knew a number of national film critics who admitted to him that they, too, hated the film, but that they came out *for it* so as not to appear to support the Falwells and Wildmons of the world! How is *that* for ethical journalism?

This journalistic skulduggery comes as no surprise to Reed Irvine, founder and chairman of Accuracy in Media, the watchdog agency that exposes the frightening bias in the American media. Irvine has found the liberal bias to be particulary strong among movie and television critics, who tend to use their power to kill films and programs that challenge their biased views. This "execution by biased criticism" was accomplished effectively with the movie *Hanoi Hilton* which showed the suffering and courage of American POW's in Vietnam. At the same time, Irvine notes, media critics boost films that support their positions even if they are filled with lies and errors. Irvine deplores this tendency of many journalists to tailor their reporting to fit their political or social objectives. He charges that most often this is done by suppressing facts and opinions that clash with their agendas, but that some go

168

so far as to report things they know to be of dubious accuracy, if not actually false!

In this media setting, it was particularly gratifying to find some real journalistic pros with both skill and ethics. These are now in our "first-ones-to-call-with-the-story" category. We don't turn to them with our information because they agree with us. Most don't. It's not because they slant the stories in our favor. None do. It's because they have a commitment to truth and fair play in journalism that honors the profession and protects the public.

I don't think anyone can fully understand the frustration of being mishandled by the press unless he has experienced it. The media always hold the trump cards. In a few moments on network television a newsperson can sow distortions that years of countering will not completely erase. Writers may print distortions on the front page, but rare retractions appear far back in the papers. Tim and I eventually would take only longer length, live interviews on radio or television, so that they couldn't leave our side of the story on the cutting room floor.

One evening on Fox Channel 11 in Los Angeles the station aired an "editorial" on the evening news ridiculing the people who were protesting *a film they hadn't seen* (sound familiar?). As the newsperson read a scathingly sarcastic piece from the teleprompter, he would pause periodically for a pianist to play a few more bars of "Three Blind Mice." This merciless ridicule ended with a belittling, "Maybe we should cut off their tales with a carving knife!" I called the station asking for a copy of the editorial. They would make none available. I inquired whether they would allow responsible spokespersons of opposing viewpoints to speak on the program. They would not. One of my staff called asking the same questions. He was told they wouldn't release their material unless it was subpoenaed! I called twice seeking a call back from the person who had delivered the piece. No calls back. Can you imagine the venom they would spew forth if someone ripped them off in this manner? Yet they sit securely on the walls of their fortresses and pour boiling oil over the edge on the innocents. What chance do the innocents have?

The media demolition crew became a far more formidable enemy at many points than the producers and distributors of a film defaming our Lord. They were formidable because they had a near monopoly on the weapons of the warfare. We had just three: truth, time, and the Divine Editor whom we trust to keep impeccable records of the way truth is handled. Without those three we would have been totally demolished early in the conflict.

After reading this chapter, you should be able to understand one of my primary motivations for writing this book! You deserve to hear the rest of the story.

10

Broadened Front

> The flap over director Martin Scorsese's *Last Temptation of Christ* has involved evangelicals, film executives, newspaper publishers and film festival organizers. Now noted Italian film director Franco Zeffirelli has stepped into the fray. Zeffirelli said Tuesday he is removing his latest work, *The Young Toscanini* . . . from the Venice Film Festival because officials there have announced they will show Scorsese's film, too. Calling his American colleague's film "truly horrible and deranged," Zeffirelli said he had "no intention whatsoever" to get mixed up in the scandals, controversies, and protests that will mark the next Venice Film Festival.
>
> - *Los Angeles Times* Morning Report,
> August 3, 1988

By the first of August, the press furor that had started as an ad in *The Hollywood Reporter* and a press conference in Ballroom C of The Registry hotel just three weeks earlier was now an international controversy.

Italian Catholics came alive with anger at the decision to show *Temptation* at the Venice Film Festival. By August 4, 45 Catholic groups across Italy had demanded the resignation of the director of the festival, Guglielmo Biraghi. The Christian Democratic party, the strongest political group in Italy, joined in demanding the resignation. With Italian film critics standing solidly behind Biraghi's decision to screen the film, Italy became a battlefield like the U. S., with the forces of the liberal media and the conservative church peering through their gunsights at each other. Franco Zeffirelli's position that the film was an insult to Catholicism was shared by millions of Italians. He declared, "I feel ashamed at the presence of an anti-religious, provocative film at the festival."[33]

Christians in Great Britain began bracing for the arrival of the film in London and other British cities. They explored the use of blasphemy laws still on the books in England to mount a legal attack on the film. In other countries around the world, especially those with strong Roman Catholic populations and Campus Crusade for Christ staff representation, believers began hearing about the U. S. controversy. In a variety of ways they prepared to mobilize protests against the film. In other instances they planned strategies to use the possible entry of the film into their countries to share evangelistic messages and stir discussion of Christ and faith in Him. The Evangelical Sisterhood of Mary continued to pray fervently and to speak out against the film in the U. S. and a number of other countries. In South Africa believers mobilized to deploy existing laws to keep the film from being imported. A representative from Campus Crusade for Christ in Germany visiting the U. S. called our office seeking counsel for a strategy for his country which would highlight an evangelistic witness to non-Christians. India and Israel later banned the film.

Meanwhile, back in the U. S. of A. the issue was ablaze in nearly every hamlet and town. All over America Christian leaders were gearing up for action. Donald

172

Wildmon, Jerry Falwell, and James Dobson had sent out millions of pieces of mail. Tens of thousands of Fact Sheets were being duplicated and distributed in church congregations. *The Hollywood Reporter* called the national situation "a tide of protest."[34] In Orlando, Florida, an interdenominational group calling itself Citizens for Decency held a noontime "prayer vigil" at Universal Studios near Disney World. Though the theme park officials said that there would be business as usual, when the protesters, estimated at between one and two thousand people, arrived at Universal, the offices were closed for the afternoon and mounted police met them.

Dr. Richard Lee, pastor of 7,000 member Rehoboth Baptist Church in the Atlanta area, began collecting the first of what became 135,000 signatures on a petition to deliver to Universal asking them not to release the film. The Church of God, America's oldest pentecostal denomination, passed a resolution condemning the film as an "attack" on Christians. The resolution was adopted unanimously by the church's General Council, conducting its biennial meeting in Forth Worth, Texas. Atlantan, Dr. Ted Baehr, president of Good News Communications which publishes *Movieguide,* the most widely distributed Christian guide to movies and entertainment, declared that the controversy could only be viewed as the culmination of years of Christian frustration with the entertainment industry. "People have said, 'enough is enough' and never will it be the same. The days of Christian bashing are over."[35]

"Christian bashing," not a household phrase in American media before this time, was a focal point in the column most quoted, duplicated, and distributed by Christians. Syndicated columnist Patrick J. Buchanan, writing in a column titled, "Hollywood's War on Christianity," quoted evangelical Christians as declaring the film "sacreligious, blasphemous, and anti-Christian."[36] "Surely they are right," declared Buchanan, "Even sight unseen, the movie represents an act of cinematic vandalism against the beliefs that Christians hold sacred; it is a deliberate profanation of the Faith. The confusing, conflicting explanations tossed out by Universal Pictures suggest a bad conscience." Buchanan's article, perhaps more than the writings of any other person, became the rallying cry of the national protest at that point in the struggle. He reacted to the emergence of Jack Valenti representing the Motion Picture Association of America. Following is the part of his column which expressed more eloquently than the words of others the sense of inequity and offense which Christians felt:

Under the First Amendment, the Protocols of the Elders of Zion are surely protected, as would be the anti-semitic Nazi tracts of Julius Streicher. Would Mr. Valenti defend their distribution by, say, Waldenbooks? Would Mr. Valenti defend a film entitled *The Secret Life of Martin Luther King,* that depicted the assassinated civil rights leader as a relentless womanizer, a point of view with more foundation in truth, and surely, less of a profanation, than showing Jesus of Nazareth as a lusting wimp? Would Mr. Valenti employ his eloquence to defend a film portraying Anne Frank as an oversexed teenager fantasizing at Auschwitz on romancing some SS guards?

Of course not.

We live in an age where the ridicule of blacks is forbidden, where anti-Semitism is punishable by political death, but where Christian-bashing is a popular indoor sport; and films mocking Jesus Christ are considered avant-garde.

Two decades ago, network television ceased showing Amos 'n' Andy reruns, ceased depicting blacks as Stepin Fetchit figures, so as not to perpetuate a stereotype Hollywood had helped to create.

With *The Last Temptation of Christ,* Hollywood is assaulting the Christian community in a way it would never dare assault the black community, the Jewish community, or the gay community.

And the reason Universal Pictures and Mr. Scorsese are doing this is because they know they can get away with it. Their Hollywood chums will laugh and whisper, "Right on! Stick it to 'em!" Their clerical camp followers at the National Council of Churches will provide the religious cover. And the controversy will guarantee big profits all around. Who cares if the Christian community is outraged, or individual Christians are hurt and offended?

"Sensitivity" is supposed to have become the mark of the man of decency in modern American life. So we are told. A "sensitive" man does not repeat ethnic jokes; he does not abide insults to any minority; he monitors his rhetoric, lest he inadvertently give offense. James Watt and Earl

Butz were driven from Cabinet seats for violating that taboo. Jimmy the Greek was fired by CBS for showing "insensitivity" in his post-prandial musings about the natural superiority of black athletes.

Christians, however, America's unfashionable majority, may be mocked; their preachers may be parodied in books and on film; their faith may be portrayed as superstitious folly. And secular society, invoking the First Amendment, will rush to the defense of the defamers, not the defamed.

The battle over *Last Temptation* is one more skirmish in the century's struggle over whose values, whose beliefs shall be exalted in American culture, and whose may be derided and disparaged.

What all of Hollywood, now rallying around Universal Pictures, is saying with its unqualified endorsement of *The Last Temptation of Christ* is: "Hey, you Christians, look here; we're showing your God and your Savior, Jesus Christ, having sex with Mary Magdalene; now, what are you going to do about it?[37]

"What Christians were going to do about it" was express themselves as never before in this century to Hollywood and, especially, to honchos in the fifteen story Power Tower at Universal City. For starters, additional millions of pieces of mail went out from Donald Wildmon's American Family Association. Wildmon's efforts to alert the nation about this film went back to the days of Scorsese's pitch to Paramount

176

in 1983, making him the "granddaddy" of the protest. "Stop Universal Studios" read the header of AFA's oversized letter. Included was a mock ticket to *Temptation* with the instructions to tear it in half, write "NO THANKS" on one half, and then stick it to a preaddressed postcard to Sid Sheinberg. Included was a petition to be signed and delivered to local theater owners, and a request for contributions to help fight the fight. Presumably hundreds of thousands followed the directions and provided a postcard shower for Sheinberg.

As always, a handful of Christians with a higher "flake factor" than others was busy seeing mystical relationships and getting mystical revelations they were using to try to spur the Body of Christ onward. Those who were even more sure than we were (and we were pretty sure) that the entire LTOC film creation originated with Lucifer, noted that one of the film's previews for the press was held in Universal's New York City screening room at *666* Fifth Avenue--and we all know who's behind those numbers!

Another well meaning, but obviously misguided, "mad scientist of the faith" laid a volume of documents on my desk seeking to prove that *The Last Temptation of Christ* release was God's "last straw unto judgment." The 25 pages of single spaced documentation built a case through prophetic revelations by some Christian brothers and sisters, a mysterious earthquake that left unusual cracks in the L. A. City Hall, and a numeral matching system which included the 777 prefixes of MCA/Universal telephones. The conclusion of all this? That a major earthquake would hit Los Angles on August 12, 1988, "followed by 40 days of warning to the L. A. populace and a mass exodus from the city led by newly

'Spirit-sensitized' Christians, including many new converts in the aftermath of the first quake, after which would come the total destruction of the city." Not being convinced, after digesting the 25 pages, that I could count on a divinely caused earthquake to swallow up Universal on the twelfth, I went back to trying to decide what God wanted other, more reasonable Christians and me to do!

The burning question was what Universal leadership was *going to do* about what Christians *were going to do.* Guess! They decided to *push up the release date of the film* 43 days to capitalize further on the heat wave of controversy and *curiosity* about this previously unsung flick! They were doing this despite telling more than one Christian leader that release dates could not be changed because of "contractual agreements!" In an announcement released by Universal on August 4, Tom Pollock announced that the September 23 release date, which we had known for weeks was phoney, would be changed to August 12--August 12, a week from the time the release hit the press! According to Pollock:

> The best thing that can be done for *The Last Temptation of Christ* at this time is to make it available to the American people and allow them to draw their own conclusions based on fact, not fallacy . . . . As Universal has said before and will say again and again until someone begins listening: Our position in this is that we are backing Martin Scorsese's vision . . . . It is his movie--we are doing this for him . . . . And in the end it will all come down to the movie. And the movie will speak for itself.[38]

The movie began to speak for itself all right. The more people who saw it, the more people there were who denounced it for a wide variety of reasons. *Time* magazine was one of the first national publications that reviewed it. The review by *Time,* August 15, 1988, still stands as one of the most balanced, most complete presentations of the *content* of the film.

> Temptation is drenched in blood. The blood of sacrified animals runs through the streets, blood unaccountably pours out of an apple Jesus eats and, at the Last Supper, the wine literally turns into blood. In one grotesque scene, Jesus reaches into His chest (though it looks more like his belly), yanks out his heart, and holds it up for his apostles to admire.
>
> For a few critics, this display seems to be an arch-sendup of the Catholic devotion to the Sacred Heart of Jesus. Some dialogue also hints at satire, probably unintentionally. Asked by a Zealot to compare being dead with being alive, the resurrected Lazarus says thoughtfully, "I was a little surprised. There isn't that much difference." At times Jesus sounds like a mumbling method actor (his first sermon beings "Umm, uh, I'm sorry"), at others like a recent graduate of the Shirley MacLaine School of Theology ("Everything's part of God").[39]

The first TV movie critic I saw speak about the film was Gary Franklin of Channel 7, ABC in Los Angeles. Franklin described the " . . . ritual animal slaughtering, which was really gross . . . It's such a borrrring

179

movie, and neither Jews or Christians should be concerned . . . ." He observed that the only people who should be offended by the film are the people who paid $6.50 to see it.   Franklin further suggested that the theaters might need more ushers--not to handle the crowds, but to keep people awake during the two hour and forty minute droner.

Michael Medved of *Sneak Previews* said, "It is the height of irony that this level of controversy could be generated by a movie this awful . . . . I can understand why the religious groups would be offended, as would the public, by this boredom."[40] "An intellectual exercise of the 'what if?' variety," said Bob Thomas of Associated Press.   "At times moving, often over-wrought, and at least 40 minutes too long."[41]

Steve Cooper of the San Bernardio *Sun* called it "The movie equivalent of a 3-inch-thick Russian novel. Should I pick up such a heavy tome? Do I care about the Great Issues of life?   How old will I be when I finish reading it? This film's like that. It's work to watch." He suggested that technically it has "severe problems." He calculated that it had been "manhandled" during editing, said it looked like it had been put together with "Band-Aids and spit."[42]

The Hollywood Reporter critic, Duane Byrge, was prophetic about the film's ultimate outcome: "Other than the street-corner Yahoo-pla, which should insure a curiosity surge on its opening weekend, Martin Scorsese's aesthetically graceless and philosophically turgid big-theme offering will be a dry hole." He called Schrader's script "manifestly a parched and trite reworking, "the dialogue making Jesus come across as "sounding like someone who's been trapped for 40 years in a Grateful Dead convoy; his numerous utterances on "love" seem as if they've been gleaned from packets advertising bath oil products rather from on high . . . . So muted and metallic sounding are Dafoe's numerous voiceovers that one is shocked into thinking the the voice of God sounds just like the Kentucky Fried Chicken order machine." Byrge describes Judas as an embodiment of "the antithesis of Jesus teachings" and strange as a red head as well. He suggests that "permed with a flaming Bozo orange do, Harvey Keitel [Judas] may be mistaken by some as the burning bush when he first appears . . . ."[43]

Warning! I am using "selective omission" in this chapter as I describe the critics. I am not including the positive reviews. You can read them in the ads Universal ran for the picture in the appendix to this book. After a week in release, the film was hyped with ads so filled with the scant positive comments from the critics that they made the film sound like a remake of *Chariots of Fire*. Some of the critics did love the movie, but my best "guesstimates" are that the comments ran about two to one against it.

The U. S. Catholic Church "critics" followed through on earlier projections with an "O" rating for "morally offensive" and "not suitable for audiences of any age." The rating statement by the Catholic bishop's Department of Communication said that "nothing can be gained by viewing it" and that it would outrage most Christians. Bishop Anthony G. Bosco of the department said, "I looked in vain for the message of love. Scorsese has given us an angry Christ, a bumbling Christ, a Christ more of this world than the next."[44]

The protest continued to be very much of *this* world.

181

As more and more people saw the film in a series of private screenings held by Universal for press and clergy (precious few conservative clergymen, thank you), and more and more critics denounced it on varied grounds, we thought things would start to move our direction. They didn't. The Moguls of MCA were obviously galvanized in their resolve to release the film *no matter what.* Even if no witness had verified Sheinberg's statement that the Christians "weren't going to stop them from releasing the film," and, even if he "never said anything like that" as he claims, his deeds were clearly outshouting his words.

With less than a week to make a final desperate attempt to change the minds of the guys with offices in the northeast corners of the Black Tower (northwest corner offices are occupied by secondary powers), those of us involved in the effort realized we had to pull out the stops, *all* the stops. Day after day for the nearly two weeks leading up to the week of the twelfth we prayed and conferred, conferred and prayed. Day after day I would ask Tim, "What do you think, Tim? Do you have any directon?" After some interaction we would mutually agree that we didn't. Many days Tim would ask me the same question, and I would give him the same answer, "No direction." We had agreed that if we didn't have what we felt was direction from God, we wouldn't move.

On Friday afternoon, August 5, I was in Tim's office, staying late to attend a hobby show in Burbank that evening before driving the hour and a half to my home. As it turned out, I missed all but the closing minutes of the show because of a "divine appointment." Tim told me that David Moore, the director of communication for the Los Angeles Catholic Archdiocese, was going to be dropping by to chat about "things," so I stayed around to spend some time interacting about the state of the battle. Dave arrived with his charming and spiritually sensitive wife, and the four of us began to pour over the LTOC situation together. Dave is a fun, transparent, and deeply committed Christian. *The Last Temptation* events had drawn us together in a special way. That evening we were enjoying each other, the weighing of the situation, and some "possibility thinking" about the warfare.

I don't remember who it was--it may have been Dave --that suggested we spend some concentrated time in prayer for God's guidance. The four of us slipped to our knees in Tim's office and the "divine appointment" occurred. The Spirit of God infused our prayers with a genuine sense of His presence. Out of that evening confab came the decision to have a second press conference on August 9--one calling for an all-out boycott of MCA/Universal and its varied business interests.

The unanimity we felt after that time of prayer made the planning easy. David would take care of notifying the press. Dave and I would both rough out possible press statements and compare them by telephone in time to edit them and get them duplicated before the conference. Mastermedia staff would set up the arrangements at The Registry for 11:00 a. m. on Tuesday and help out with press notification as needed. Dave would have his people bring lights for the camera people, so that some camera crew wouldn't pack up early taking its lights along and leaving the room dark as happened near the end of the July 12 conference. The evening spent, we headed out to our various weekend assignments.

The press conference was the most ecumenical affair I have ever attended, much less helped orchestrate. I considered sending the troika at MCA/Universal a "thank you" note for helping to bring such a diverse group of Christians together! The interaction in the briefing room before the press conference was getting a little zooy when the bell rang on round one of the conference. Turn loose ten religious leaders with a page and a half written statement they haven't seen before and each one turns into a word surgeon. Bill Bright and Mother Angelica teamed up to quell the interaction between a Baptist and a bishop with the statement, "if we can't agree in this room, we have no business going out to face the press!"

The conference participants, whom you will meet shortly, opened the event with a short time of silent prayer. Tim read the statement which summarized the degeneration of the relationship with Universal since the last press conference, described the incredible breadth of the national protest, and highlighted the Black Tower's response:

> To all of this outcry MCA/Universal executives have turned a deaf ear. To the offer to purchase they responded that American freedoms were not for sale, as if they owned them. To the many expressions of offense there has not been one apology nor one indication of regret. To the requests for the film's withdrawal they have moved full speed ahead toward the film's release and have even expanded the release to worldwide markets."

The statement concluded by proclaiming a three-fold message:

1) *All of us* here call for all Americans to refuse to patronize the showing of the film.

2) *A majority of us* here call for a refusal to patronize for one year from August 12, 1988, any business interest of MCA/Universal or its subsidiaries *and* any local theater or chain of theaters choosing to screen the film.

3) *Some of us* are calling for measures that are more or less stringent than those of the majority.

That last call was a "catch all" to include a couple of the participants who felt either that the boycott should not include *all* MCA business interests or who thought that it should continue *forever!*

Going alphabetically, Mother Angelica, foundress of the Eternal Word Television Network, served as "lead off" batter. Wearing her brown habit, frequently clutching the wooden crucifix around her neck, and expressing the deepest of emotion, she indicated she was wearing a black arm band of mourning for "the spiritual death of apathetic Christians and Catholics who stand by and watch the Lord God, Jesus Christ, Savior maligned, blasphemed, made to seem a fool--a wimping fool." She predicted that those who would knowingly go to the film, aware of its blasphemous content, would "commit the sin against the Holy Spirit."

Father John Bartke of St. Michael's Orthodox Church reminded the press that Nikos Kazantzakis was both excommunicated and refused burial in his native Greece by his church, the Orthodox Church, because of the book. He regretted that his church now had to "face this matter again as a movie." He stated his opposition to the attack on any religious group by a film such as this and called on the six million members of the Orthodox churches in America to refuse to attend the movie. He expressed hope that Universal would "have a change of heart" and not release the movie.

Campus Crusade for Christ's founder and president, Bill Bright, noted that a recent Gallup Poll indicated that 84% of the American people believe in the deity of Jesus Christ. He observed that "the offense of this tragic film would be heartbreak for tens of millions" who believe in Christ. He expressed confidence that this tragedy could be turned to triumph if "millions of believers would take the opportunity to share with others the historical/biblical Christ." He presented a booklet that could be used for this purpose.

Christian radio personality Rich Buhler then took the podium to express his concern. Rich's large frame, ample beard, and safari suit trademark set him apart from the other participants. Rich predicted that the release of *The Last Temptation of Christ* would be "one of the greatest miscalculations of American history." He continued, "In more than 25 years of Los Angeles media I have never seen more of a consensus among intelligent and sober Christians than I have regarding this film." He likened Universal's response to Christ and Christians to an obscene street gesture.

Tim Penland relayed the dramatic story of Tom Pollock's plea for help and his expressed desire to release a "faith affirming" film that would not blaspheme Jesus Christ. He recounted how Christian leaders had basically given Universal five months of peace in a gesture of good faith. Tim then called on Tom Pollock to make good on his promises and not release the film.

Radiant and reflecting a kind of innocent aura in her protestant clerical garb, Sister Rebekka of the Evangelical Sisterhood of Mary read a statement from Mother Basilea Schlink, the founder of this movement of repentance in Germany and a woman who has stood against other cinematic attacks on Christ. The statement affirmed the deity, purity and holiness of Jesus Christ and called the film "one of the most underhanded deceptions and blasphemies the world has ever seen . . . . Bible passages are misused and interwoven with obscenities to make it a most degrading and distorted picture of Jesus Christ." She reminded the world that the Book of Galatians declares "one cannot make a fool of God."

Bishop John J. Ward, Auxiliary Bishop from the L. A. Roman Catholic archdiocese, strode deliberately to the podium and began to speak in bursts of well-chosen words delivered in deep, well-rounded tones. He called the film not "the last temptation" but "the ultimate exploitation of the greatest character in all of human history . . . for greed." He indicated that the church was choosing to follow the "eyeball witnesses to the life of Christ--Matthew, John--not the dreams and fiction of a man in the twentieth century." He called for the Christian community to send a message to the media community that we would not meet this offense with impunity.

The Southern Baptist Convention, 14 million strong nationwide, was represented by Thomas Wolf of the California Baptist Convention. Tom declared the film to

187

be (1) morally grotesque because of the portrayal of Christ, (2) a historical affront because of the clear violation of the historical record, not because of artistic license, (3) religiously offensive, even if done to any other religous group, and (4) socially inflammatory against Christians. The national president of the Southern Baptist convention, Dr. Jerry Vines, sent a statement calling for a boycott of the film.

I spoke on the response of believers inside the film and television industries, stating that the issue had changed substantially since the first press conference. I declared that the issue of the film's content had been overshadowed by the issue of *Universal's response* to the pleas by millions of Christians. I observed that there was "probably no more flagrant rejection of public opinion in the history of corporate America." To Universal I pled, "Please, please hear us. You are reaping disaster on yourselves financially if you alienate so many millions who in gracious and reasonable ways in the last four weeks have expressed themselves to you."

Robert Ziener, the National Chairman of Rosaries for Peace, read a statement from Mother Teresa of Calcutta, 1979 Nobel Peace Prize winner and foundress of the Missionaries of Charity. She declared that she had written to Martin Scorsese to tell him that, as a Catholic under the authority of the Church, he could do what he was doing only if he received the permission of Cardinal O'Connor of New York. She added a "message to America: . . . pray, pray, pray! . . . prayer is the ultimate weapon to fight this ultimate disgrace."

Pray we did. But, with the countdown at T minus two

days and counting, our range of options was narrowing.

One would have thought that some higher power had known the precise release date of the film in advance and had orchestrated from foreknowledge an event which turned out to be one of the most powerful expressions of all to Universal and Hollywood. The stunning non-coincidence was that long before the organizers of the event knew Universal was going to move the release up from September 23 to August 12, they scheduled for August 11 a major public rally and press conference. Universal, by moving up the release date, had unknowingly cooperated beautifully in a divinely scheduled sequence of events.

By mid morning on August 11 people began streaming into the area surrounding the Black Tower and filling the sidewalks and streets. Cars formed serpentine chains onto freeway offramps and onto the surface streets of Universal City. Busses, vans and pickups began to unload picket signs which would spread into a field of cardboard wildflowers across every square yard of empty space around Universal and be carried thoughout the noon hour. These signs told much of the story of those marching: "Try Jesus," "He was crucified once for all," "Jesus Christ is Lord. Please show repect for my God," " The lie costs $6.50; the truth is free," "Boycott Universal," "First Amendment ≠ slander," "The almighty buck shouldn't compete with the Almighty!" "Forgive them, Father," "Jesus Christ: Fact not fiction," "Jesus is alive," "Let my Jesus alone," "Don't distort HIS-story," "Judas then, Universal Now."

By noon the masses of people so filled the area around Universal that all traffic was at a standstill. The area

189

was so clogged with traffic that police closed freeway offramps backing up traffic, some reports said, as much a eighteen miles. The air above Universal was filled with police helicopters trying to keep an eye on the situation and news helicopters catching aerial shots of the growing numbers of people. Still the crowds came--on foot, hitchiking, anyway they could get to the base of MCA/Universal's awesome Tower of Power. Camera crews from all over Southern California descended on the area. Universal's parking garage did an additional $4,000 of business for the day with every space taken, the last money the Big U would make from many of those people--ever.

As the ranks of the committed grew, they passed five thousand in number. Singing, praying, and chanting "Boycott MCA! Boycott MCA!" they filled every available cranny around the entrance to the Universal Studios tour. Their numbers passed ten thousand. There was a festive atmosphere, possibly like the reception after the Marriage Supper of the Lamb. People hugged each other, shared loving words, and moved in orderly fashion in milling circles, purposeful lines, and restful positions. The numbers grew past twenty thousand! Clutching small children, pushing baby strollers, holding hands, arm in arm, most with some kind of hand fashioned placard resting on a supporting stick on their shoulders, they moved as one toward MCA/Universal Headquarters.

Their numbers passed *twenty-five thousand!!* They were not a mob, or even a crowd, they were a family. They were God's forever family, wounded and hurting over the assault on their Heavenly Father and His Son, but sufficiently filled with the Spirit to see beyond the offense to the joy of the ultimate victory.

190

This great event brought together churches of every conceivable type, the staff of Christian organizations, carpools of believers from the beach areas, and an assortment of faithful humanity as diverse as the citizens of Heaven. Since KKLA Christian radio in Los Angeles was one of the prime movers in putting together the march and rally, John Stewart, law professor and program host on the station, called an open air press conference to order. Behind him was a linear mosaic of those who had something to say to the watching world. As Stewart began, people in the Black Tower--some terrorized by the prospect of being surrounded by 25,000 people who could shut off entry ways and storm the doors if they desired--peered apprehensively down on the multicolored ocean of God's children.

John faced the crowd with innocence in his countenance and called Universal's action "The most stunning display of religious bigotry in recent memory." He cautioned that ". . . artistic license gives no one the right to grieviously offend an entire faith of people any more than a driver's license allows one the freedom to drive while intoxicated." He called for a national boycott. He said he represented "Citizens for a Universal Appeal," a broadly based Southern California coalition of believers.

Donald Wildmon, a long way from his hometown in Tupelo, Mississippi, was obviously pleased to see the success of one of his dreams--holding Universal accountable--coming true. At the bundles of microphones Donald warned like a major prophet, "Universal says they are releasing a movie. In fact they are unleashing a movement!" Cheers from the family. "Christian bashing is over! The time when

191

Hollywood can ridicule our faith and our values and now even our God is *over!*" Subconsciously gesturing to the top of the tower, he declared, "You may not respect our religion, but you will respect our pocketbook. And we *will* express our faith in the marketplace!" More cheers and "Amen's."

By the time Trinity Broadcasting Network's Paul Crouch faced this ad hoc congregation, it was "trackin'." Members of the Body of Christ were reading from the same score as their leaders. So Paul declared the Christian's love for the leaders at MCA/Universal and called on them not to release the film "in their best interests." Quoting from the book of Hebrews, Paul called on them "not to trample underfoot the Son of God" and reminded them that it is "a fearful thing to fall into the hands of an angry God." Applause.

The parade of speakers continued to file to the microphones. Ken Wales, veteran film producer and a sensitive Christian, declared, "As a member of this industry I wish that there were hundreds of stars and writers and directors standing here with me. I suppose they are out protesting toxic waste! Let me tell you there is toxic waste and pollution in other areas besides our rivers. That happens in the pollution of our minds, our souls, and our spirits!"

Rich Buhler, beloved radio counselor on KBRT, another station heavily involved in covering the protest and promoting the rally, offered, "I don't consider Universal an enemy. I consider it a friend that has betrayed me. And I can speak for thousands and maybe even millions for whom the word "Universal" has become a stench in our nostrils. We call upon Universal to make a decision of conscience and, if not that, then a decision of economics."

Jane Chastain, a woman of considerable physical and spiritual attractiveness, stood representing Concerned Women of America. She was visual relief from the dreariness of the all-male procession. As a former sportscaster in a man's world, Jane delivered her message as if at the half time show at the super bowl: "We find Universal's First Amendment argument as a mandate for releasing this film an insult to the intelligence of the American people . . . . We are appalled that a company like Universal Studios would distort anyone's religion for the purpose of making a profit . . . . We find this insulting not only for Christians but for all Americans who abhor bigotry . . . . We will boycott everything connected with Universal and MCA. Let's make this the worst year in Universal's financial history!"

Campus Crusade's Bill Bright spoke differently from the way he had spoken at the two earlier press conferences. He obviously had experienced a "release of the spirit" from the anger and hurt that had kept him awake for weeks since reading the Schrader script. He announced that he was ". . . increasingly excited! Three days after Jesus was crucified on the cross claiming to be the Son of God, He was raised from the dead. We are here today as a testimony of His living presence. He is alive! He is being crucified by evil men once again, and this time I believe His resurrection will result in literally multitudes--tens and perhaps hundreds of millions--coming to know Jesus . . . . What man intended for evil, God will ultimately use for His good and glory!" Bill once again presented the booklet describing the true Christ.

A surprising addition to the event was the appearance of two prominent members of the Jewish community. One, Rabbi Chaim Asa, senior rabbi of a Jewish temple in Fullerton, California, somewhat nervously but clearly shared his reason for being at the rally. With a heavy European accent he asserted that he had come to ". . . join in protesting the indignity of this particular attempt to defame your God . . . . Millions across the country are saying, 'You are touching something very deep, very sensitive in my soul. Please don't do it, because this is not fair.' I protest vehemently, as many of my Christian friends did when someone tried to burn down our temple in Fullerton, California . . . . I will try to express to my Christian friends--if their pain is deep now, so is my pain for them." Warm, warm applause.

Rosey Grier, former NFL lineman, reborn Christian, and gentle giant, decried the lack of respect that now floods our country--disrespect for the President and others in authority. "Now we find a movie company that would dare to make fun of the Creator of the Universe!" Rosey agonized. "What we have to say is that we as Christians will not stand back and allow this to continue! We call for it to end now! We will use everthing that we have--and the greatest thing that we have to offer is our lives--to stop it. It has to stop, and it will stop now!" Ovation upon ovation.

My "Awesome Content Award" for the occasion went to the other representative of the Jewish community, Dennis Prager, columnist for the Los Angeles *Herald Examiner* and KABC radio personality. With his distinguished grey hair and somewhat angular face positioned high above the speaking desk, he explained that he was a committed Jew and the author of two books on Judaism. He introduced the outline of his reasons for being at this Christian rally with a quote from Rabbi Harold Schulweis, "There are core areas in each religion that should remain untouched, especially by outsiders."

In a logical progression of thought, Prager proclaimed, "It is not for people of no faith or of another faith to play with the sacred beliefs of others' faiths . . . . Martin Scorsese did not have to work out his theologial problems using the man regarded as lord and savior by hundreds of millions of people [overwhelming applause] . . . I consider this a God-given opportunity --and I emphasize God-given--for Jews and Christians to help each other . . . . The great division in America today is not between Jews and Christians but between *religious* Jews and Christans on the one hand and an agressive secularism on the other--a secularism that has overtaken the school, the home, the theater, the media, and now attempts even to overtake religion itself! Jews and Christians should have understood long before *The Last Temptation of Christ* that nearly everything that their religions hold sacred has been profaned in the movies. The issue is not Christian censorship, it is Hollywood's nihilism. If that is understood, *The Last Temptation of Christ* will actually have served a purpose."

For sheer drama, no moment at the conference surpassed the contribution of Steve Gooden, a recording artist with MCA records. The fine featured, average sized, black man could be mistaken for pop singer Michael Jackson. Immediately upon taking the mikes, he gave "glory and honor to God." Then he explained that in February he had signed a multi-year recording contract with MCA which included a single and a nine album option. He shared how he had resolved in recent weeks, upon learning of *The Last Temptation of Christ,* that he couldn't keep that contract because he wanted to use his talent "beyond ego and financial gain." He wanted to stand in a "cause against Satan." He challenged others to "stand for a righteous cause--to put convictions for Christ ahead of their own personal gain." Whereupon Steve held up his MCA contract for all to see. Proclaiming, "I tear this contract in the name of my Lord Jesus Christ," Steve ripped it in pieces! Standing ovation. Tears. In a postscript to this dramatic act he proclaimed tearfully, "I'm not a big celebrity, but this is what I can do." As the ovation deafened those nearby, Steve Gooden was engulfed in the arms of giant Rosie Grier.

In a town where "bigger is better," 25,000 people united against one studio was a great statement. Hollywood was stunned. Beefed up security forces at Universal breathed a sigh of release as the protesters packed up their picket signs and went home--without one ugly incident or arrest. A lawsuit prepared by Cineplex Odeon for filing--should leaders of the protest do violence to persons or property--went unused. The snaking vehicles inched their way through the artificial freeway rush hour to their homes.

Homeward bound, weary believers were taunted by the bold faced copy in double page ads in the major dailies:

**"MARTIN SCORSESE,
AMERICA'S MOST GIFTED,
MOST DARING MOVIEMAKER,
MAY HAVE CREATED HIS MASTERPIECE."
- Richard Corliss, TIME MAGAZINE**

**On Friday, August 12,
one of the great
filmmakers of our
time brings us
a startling vision.**

**An extraordinary story,
based on the highly
acclaimed novel by
Nikos Kazantzakis.**

THE LAST
TEMPTATION
OF CHRIST

11

Universal Offense

Even if the sun was coming up on the east side of the globe as it always did, even if the mountains outside my living room windows didn't appear to have moved a silly millimeter, there was something very different about this day. It was August 12, 1988.

In Italy Catholic Archbishop Marcel Lefebvre presumably went about his daily business unaware that what was happening in Century City, California, would change his life as it would. In France, Cardinal Albert Decourtray, archbishop of Lyon, was no doubt attending to the business of the church without realizing that he would be affected significantly by a decision executed in Universal City. Church of England clergyman, Rev. Dr. William Oddie, could not have known that August 12 would be the launch of a film he would ultimately have to denounce as "bad beyond belief . . . both theologically offensive and artistically incompetent."[45] But in 30 days all three of these men would be involved in international denunciations of *The Last Temptation of Christ*--not from hearsay, but by eyewitness of the movie on screens *in their own countries.*

The full page and double, full page ads had been running for a couple of days in all the major newspapers. Graphically stylized thorns filled large portions of the ads. At the bottom of each, **"UNIVERSAL PICTURES AND CINEPLEX ODEON FILMS PRESENT "THE LAST TEMPTATION OF CHRIST."** During the day the letters went up on the marquee of the Cineplex

Odeon theater in Century City, a modern metropolis built on what used to be the back lot of 20th Century Fox. This was the day the final stage of earthly accountability would begin for those in the seats of power at MCA, Universal Pictures, and Cineplex Odeon. This was August 12.

Tim and I both confessed later that we woke up "down" that day. As we talked it through, we recognized it was *grief*. It wasn't a sense of *defeat*, the numbing and silent sensation that grips you while walking out of the championship game your team lost by one point in the final seconds.   It wasn't *anger* like the inner turbulence you experience when you have just received an unjust attack on your ego or your reputation and are helpless to defend yourself. It wasn't *weariness*, the mental, emotional, and spiritual tiredness that marks the first hour after a marathon. It was *grief*. It was what I felt watching those hideous slow motion replays of John Kennedy's head being shattered by bullets in Dallas. It was what I felt flying back to Indiana to bury my mother a few years ago. It was what I felt a few weeks ago as I embraced my friend whose wife had been killed in a head-on collision. It was *grief*.

As I write this, that same feeling has come back. The unexplainable ache somewhere between my heart and my lungs. The tightness across the forehead signalling an impending headache. The unmistakably "sick" feeling near the solar plexis which I know won't result in vomiting but I almost wish would. It has a portion of that bittersweet urge I feel when love consumes me in quantities greater than I can express. It's as inexpressible as the emotion I sense when embracing my four year old and wanting to "squeeze him into a love lump." It's like the desperation to break free that I once felt when I was held underwater without breath. It is an untouchable pain. It is grief.

Today is August 12. The Person that I have loved since I knelt as a five year old in front of a church in Mansfield, Ohio, is being slandered today. The One I gave up architecture to serve in 1956 while on a park bench in Bremerhaven, Germany, is being smeared today. The Person I have turned to each day for four decades is being maligned today. The Man who understands my temptations because He experienced them, but resisted so He could help me do the same, is being lied about today. The God I turn to to forgive and cleanse me is being sinned against by somebody else today. Today is August 12.

As Tim and I talked about it, we imagined the first dollar bill handed through a theater window somewhere in the country signifying that Universal *really* had done it. We envisioned some cosmic gavel being driven by the Judge of the Universe into His desk to pronounce sentence. It seemed to us as if thirty pieces of silver were peanuts compared to the millions that soon would be paid by folks who would support this kind of cinematic betrayal of the life and message of Jesus. From now on it was out of our hands. We had done everything we found humanly possible and had trusted God to do anything divinely permissible to persuade Universal not to bring the consquences of August 12 on them. But they had consummated the offense.

Many of us had worked longer hours, prayed more urgent prayers, made more phone calls, planned more strategies, spoken more words of persuasion, and expended more BTU's of emotional and spiritual energy

200

on this than most anything else in our lives. As we looked backward over our shoulders and peered forward over the horizon, we saw the ingredients of a universal offense.

The Offense Against Ethics

It wasn't a big deal to Tim or me that we had been ripped off in a premeditated assault by the top executives of a giant American corporation. In all fairness, we asked for it. We calculated from the very first that we might be being "set up" by Universal for its own nefarious purposes. At every junction of the circuitous journey through the jungles of MCA, we realized the very real possibility that this train would take us to some destination other than the one the conductor had described to us. We were so very aware of this that we stayed near an open door, ready to exit our contractual Pullman at all times.

This book is not a "don't get mad, get even" treatise. We aren't angry, we're disappointed--disappointed that the corporate motivations and operations of such a significant U. S. business would be so characterized by ethical poverty.

One of the lightning bolts we received late in the game came on a call from Pat Broeske of the *Los Angeles Times*. Pat had had a conversation with Marian Billings, the head of Scorsese's publicity firm in New York, about *Temptation.* When Pat asked about the role Universal and Scorsese had had in mind for Tim Penland, Marian said, "Oh, he was a decoy." Not a little stunned with this response, Pat pursued, "Are you saying *on the record* that Tim Penland was hired to decoy opposition to the film from Christians?" "That's

201

right," Ms. Billings replied.[46] That sounded a whole lot different from the "bridges to the Christian community" line Tim had heard. It was worlds away from the "faith affirming film" representations given to Tim by Universal and Scorsese. And it bore scant resemblance to the concept of holding screenings for Christian leaders to "gain their input."

I remember the day in June that we talked with a reporter for the *Chicago Tribune* who had discovered the "secret" screening for Universal's distribution people in New York, the one that took place long before the public one for religious leaders on July 12. He told us of the repeated denials he was receiving from the agents of U. P. "I'm not accustomed to being lied to," he said, "People don't lie to the *Chicago Tribune*. We are going to hold them accountable for this."

One of the most flagrant examples of duplicity spilling out of Universal City occurred in communication between California Senator H. L. "Bill" Richardson's office and Tom Pollock's. Senator Richardson, impressed by the many calls from his constituents expressing ire over the impending release of LTOC, decided that he would introduce a resolution in the California legislature holding Universal accountable. Before he drafted any resolution, the Senator thought it best to request a screening, so that he and cosponsoring legislators could be sure they knew what they were talking about.

Richardson's aide at the time, Mike Carrington, called the Tower to reach board chairman Tom Pollock. He had difficulty getting anything but a busy signal, but finally got through. Carrington asked for Tom Pollock's office and was transferred internally. A male voice answered and said that Mr. Pollock was out of the country. The man, who identified himself as "Bret," assured Mike, "I can help you. I'm his [Pollock's] secretary." Mike indicated that he was calling from the legislator's office and desired to set up a screening for himself, some other legislators, and key religious leaders. They chatted amiably about the arrangements, and Bret displayed rather complete information, *inside* information about the *Temptation* situation. Bret assured Mike that he could set up a screening. He said all he needed were the names of the proposed attendees and the date they would like to see it. Mike gave him that information, and Bret gave him an inside phone number.

Mike Carrington followed up shortly thereafter and got the same Bret--who had strangely become a different person. This "new" Bret indicated that "things had changed," that there was "a new policy" in effect, and that there would be "no further screenings until Martin delivered the finished film." He denied statements he had made in earlier conversations. He denied that there had been a screening in New York for distribution people.

Mike said, "Look, I can give you the time, the place, and the names of the people who attended. Don't tell me there wasn't any screening!" Bret still denied it and said Mike would have to "write Mr. Huston in Public Relations." Carrington was steamed. Veteran senators recognize doubletalk when they hear it. He demanded a satisfactory response.

A little later Mike got a call from a woman in publicity at Universal. Guess who. Sally Van Slyke! The word had apparently gotten around that Senator Richardson's office was ticked off. Sally asked what she could do to help. When Mike said he had been assured that a screening for legislators and key religious leaders was being set up, Sally didn't know anything about it and seemed troubled. She said Mr. Pollock didn't have a secretary named Bret. She indicated that Pollock was not out of the country. On the screening, she expressed, vaguely, that they "might be able to work something out." Sally denied that there had been a screening in New York for distribution people! She also denied there were plans to advance the release date.

It soon became obvious to Senator Richardson that his office was being given the run around and to pursue a screening was useless.

Much later, in a final attempt to unravel the "Who was Bret?" mystery, Mike called his number again until he got through. This time a woman answered who said the line was a referral number from the main switchboard that handled calls for Tom Pollock's "office."

While this was happening to Senator Richardson, lobbyists for the film industry elsewhere in Sacramento were furious at Universal. Having already acquired some major tax breaks for the industry and being close to getting more, *Temptation* put their efforts back into the dark ages.

The Offense Against the Value of Humans

If there is one value that has transcended religious belief in the American tradition, it is the value of the individual human being. The Bill of Rights is predicated on this premise--as is suffrage, emancipation, and a hundred other facets of the

American Way of Life. But in the scrape over *The Last Temptation* it became clear that some human beings had more or less value than others and that *Christian* human beings were at the bottom of that pecking order.

I intentionally omitted from the description of the August 11 rally the story of Rehoboth Baptist Church in the Atlanta area of Georgia. When word of LTOC reached Rehoboth's pastor, Dr. Richard G. Lee, he recognized that his people wanted to express their anger and protest at the decision of Universal to release *Temptation*. He decided to take out two ads in the *Atlanta Journal and Constitution* which said, "If you stand against this movie, sign this ad."

The reponse was overwhelming. Shortly, he had 30,000 names on the petition which he had promised to deliver to Universal. The numbers swelled to twice that amount quickly as friends and friends of friends signed, duplicated, and passed on copies of the petition. With the numbers running over 100,000, Dr. Lee began trying to contact MCA/Universal to arrange for a representative to receive the presentation of the signatures. Dr. Lee and his representatives called over and over again seeking someone in the organization who cared enough about the public, cared enough about public relations, cared enough about future business, cared enough about *anything* sufficiently to give a few minutes of time to receive the petitions.

In Pastor Lee's own words we hear Universal's answer:

> We contacted their offices, and in our last conversation last Friday, they told us, 'We don't care about your petitions. Leave them with the guards, and we'll put them in the

205

dump.' They were saying 'we don't care about the opinions and the heartbeat of 135,000 Americans' . . . . They can be *made* to care about them. If we can't speak to their hearts and we can't speak to their heads, we can speak to their wallets. Do it in love, but let's do it.[47]

Cineplex Odeon, the theater chain half owned by MCA/Universal, demonstrated similar inhumanity to those pleading with it not to screen the film. Garth Drabinsky, C.O.'s top dog, calculated ways to exploit the hurts, the anger, and the protests of millions and turn them into further profits for the company. I wouldn't be able to give you this inside picture if it had not been for a man I'll call "Bob."

I met Bob the evening of August 12 at the first evening screenings of LTOC at the Cineplex Odeon theater at Century City. After a day of grief over the launching of the film, I joined a group from our church which was going down to the theater to picket. I had been unable to attend the mass rally on the eleventh, so I was eager to see what opening night was like and to translate my hurt into some constructive, public expression.

The number of protesters was small, perhaps three hundred, and the ticket lines stretched far around the building. The patrons obviously far outnumbered the protesters. While this was disappointing to me, I had to remember that large demonstrations at theaters were never the plan. We knew that this would significantly swell the box office take.

After half an hour or more walking around with a picket sign, dodging TV crews who had come to photograph the "mass demonstration" that hadn't happened, I was giving thought to heading home. As I began to look around for those who had come in my van, I noticed my comrade from the Mastermedia staff, Buster Holmes, talking to a mid-to-late twenties guy with dark, wavy hair, white, open collared shirt, and a walkie talkie. Buster had had Bob engaged in conversation for some time when I walked up.

Buster broke off his line of conversation as I approached and said, "Bob, I'd like you to meet Larry." The following dialogue represents our recollection of the conversation that ensued.

"Nice to meet you, Bob. You working security here tonight?"

"No, not really," Bob replied. "This is our film."

"Oh, do you work for the theater?" I inquired.

"No, I work for Cineplex Odeon. We own half of this film."

Buster and I exchanged a knowing glance. "What do you do for Cineplex Odeon?" I probed.

"I work in marketing out of the L. A. office."

Bells and whistles began to go off in my brain. If Bob would talk, this could be a wonderful source of information! Buster had been playing dumb with Bob about the whole *Temptation* flap in hopes of learning anything that could help our cause. Bob couldn't have been more ready to talk. It was as if he felt important with these two religious characters asking patronizing questions of the big man in marketing with C. O.

"Bob," I began, "you said this was your film. I thought Universal owned at least half."

"Well, yeah, Universal owns half and Cineplex owns half--well actually Scorsese has part of it, too."

"Oh, really, how much did he put it in?"

"Well, Scorsese and Cineplex each put in about a third for the production and Universal put in a matching amount for distribution."

"Really? About how much did that amount to each?" I was having a tough time suppressing my excitement.

"About twelve million total." He explained that the participation was not exactly in thirds and provided some other information about the financial structuring of the deal.

"You must be thrilled with the sellout crowds here tonight," I said with mock enthusiasm. "I bet this will go on for, what, maybe two or three weeks?"

Bob looked at me like I'd just turned purple. "Are you kidding? We'll be lucky if this lasts five days!"

"What? I figured it would last longer than that!"

"No way. This film has no market. Kids won't go to it. Familes won't go to it. It's a dog. It's an art film. We never expected it to play anywhere but art film theaters. If it hadn't been for all this attention, it wouldn't be here."

"So what's the plan for distributing the film?"

"Well, we opened in just one theater in each city to focus the attention on the theaters. This way we get maximum publicity. See these protesters here? If you divided those among even five theaters, do you think the press would be out here?"

I began to see the careful calculation behind the strategy, calculation that obviously had *not one thought* for the sensitivies of those earnest people carrying placards, chatting with the people in lines, singing Christian songs. Cineplex wouldn't have cared if the protesters were gays, socialists, environmentalists, or the humane society--just so long as they swelled the box office. I felt myself getting a little stirred inside.

Bob continued. "Then, after the attendance has peaked, we'll 'shotgun' the film into a lot of cities trying to skim off the curiosity factor and then bag it. We want to get rid of this film. The guys upstairs don't like it. It's a headache." Bob shifted hands on his walkie talkie.

"What's the walkie talkie for?" I asked.

"It's so I can talk to the bosses. They all flew in from Toronto to see what they might have to deal with in other cities where we open. You see that hotel across the street? They're sittin' up there watching the whole thing. I'm supposed to let them know what's happening down here--you know, any violence or anything. What a joke! These people are harmless. They've mostly been singing. They sing 'Jesus Loves Me,' so I call 'em and say, 'Now they're singing 'Jesus Loves Me'.'" Buster and I laughed. If Bob had known what we were thinking, he would have known we were chuckling more at Bob's "free info" than his "singing reports."

"We've got our own camera crew here, too. Out there on the median strip."

We looked in the direction Bob was pointing to see a large tripod with a film camera atop it.

"We're getting footage to use in the film's promotion, especially for international distribution." The stirring in me turned to irritation. I pictured this attack on my Lord in some of the seventy countries in which I had labored for eight and a half years to take the *true* story of Jesus Christ.

"Like, if we open in Sweden, instead of showing just the preview clips of the film, we'll show pictures of the protests. We're thinking of saying, 'Come see the film that brought American Christians out of the closet!'"

The irritation inside me turned to anger. First they trample on the sensitivities and deep beliefs of millions by shoving the film down their throats. Then they manipulate the protests in every way they can to swell the gate from the hurt and angry people that express themselves. Then they export the offense to *international markets.* Finally, they exploit the protestors further by using pictures of their heartfelt expressions to draw others into their snare with *"Come see the film that brought American Christians out of the closet!"* And the Cineplex big wigs fly into L. A. to watch the spectacle from a high rise hotel balcony as if they were watching the Lions eat Christians in the Coliseum!

That was enough. Buster and I wrapped up the talk, and

I impishly gave him a Mastermedia business card "to pass along." We regrouped for the trip home. I was angry, but not at Bob. This wasn't Bob's fault, after all, he was an underling in the heartless conspiracy--"Come see the film . . ." kept flashing on the screen of my mind, ". . . that brought American Christians out of the closet!" This was a big game of chess to them! They cared *not at all* about faith, feelings, hurts, injury, eternal salvation or damnation. They had *business* to conduct.

Have you heard even ONE expression of apology, regret, solace, empathy, sympathy, or concern emanating from the heart of the Black Tower or from the Cineplex HQ in Toronto? None. Nein. Zip. Zilch. They just *do not care*.

The Offense Against Conscience

I can picture myself in numerous situations over the years apologizing to others who expressed to me that they were "hurt" by me when I had no intent to hurt them, wouldn't have hurt them for the world, didn't have a clue that any malfeasance or misfeasance of mine was creating injury, and, basically, didn't feel I had any obligation to apologize. Yet, it seemed the right thing to do to protect the relationship and heal their bruised spirits, their injured consciences.

Where was that tenderness, that sensitivity at MCA? At Universal? At Cineplex Odeon? If we could have any *quantitative* measure of the flood of sincere expressions that reached the MCA conglomerate, it would be staggering--it would number in the millions. But that measure would no more reflect the injury created by Hollywood's leadership than the recital of

211

the empty statistics of war dead. Unless you realize that every war dead digit represents a hurt family, a lost loved one, a network of broken hearts, the statistics are hollow.

Before Tim Penland terminated his relationship with Universal, Pollock, Kornblitt, and Van Slyke passed along a sampling of those letters. Read each of the following letters and multiply it by 100,000. Maybe then you will gain a feel for the magnitude of the offense.

Handwritten by Mr. and Mrs. C. R., Pocatella, Idaho:

Universal Studios
Louis Wasserman,

This is a letter to inform you that I ask you not to release the movie "The Last Temptation of Christ." Our family and others will not watch it (and get others to do the same). You are putting a bad name on yourself if you let the movie be released.

The subject matter of the movie personally bothers me. It contradicts everything the Bible teaches. We ask you not to release this movie.

Thank you,

Mr. and Mrs. C. R.

Personally typed, grammatically weak, two page letter:

Dear Mr. Wasserman:

I understand you're releasing a movie around March of '88 depicting our LORD JESUS Christ as an adulterer. Who are you trying to bamboozle? This is heresy and blasphemy, and I, for one, being a Christian, cannot and will not remain silent. In fact, I'm quite indignant . . . . Jesus Christ Himself claimed to be God incarnate as it is written in the book of John chapter 8 verse 58. Jesus also said, "You will die IN YOUR SINS UNLESS you believe that I AM." But the good news is that God so loves you, Mr. Wasserman, that he gave His only son that whoever believes in Him shall not perish but have eternal life." It is a fact that the death rate is still one per person. We must all die some time. But the question is, "Will Jesus be your judge or savior? . . . . And in closing I would like to say, Jesus said, "I AM the way, and the truth, and the life; no one comes to the Father but through me.

In love sincerely,

B. J.

P.S.
Call on the name of the Lord while He may be found. Seek Him while he is near. Isaiah 55 verse 6.

Nicely typed, grammatically correct, one page letter to Lou Asserman [Sic]:

Dear Sir:

This is to inform you of our opposition to the release of the movie called "The Last Temptation of Christ."

It is our understanding that this movie was taken from a novel of similar title. If Jesus Christ is portrayed as anything other than the perfect son of God, we would not find the movie entertaining or of any social significance.

The Bible gives us the written record of four eyewitness accounts of the nature and character of the life of Jesus Christ. We know of no opposing written records. A movie based on a 20th century novel would seem to be slanderous and blaphemous to our Lord and Savior Jesus Christ.

He is the only hope we have of salvation from the effects of sin and death.

Peace in Christ,

Dr. and Mrs. D. L

Poorly handwritten letter with many spelling and grammatical errors:

Dear Mr. Wasserman:

I hope that this is the first of the thousands of letters which will be flocking to your office in the next few weeks to come. I just got news today . . . of the fact that your organization has purchased the rights to a movie depicting our LORD & SAVIOR as a common, sinful, mere man. Maybe you don't believe it (obviously), but the Bible says that He was pure & spotless, the only sacrifice which our FATHER in HEAVEN would accept as the atonement or substitute for man's sinful and despairing nature . . . . If you had what we have, Mr. Wasserman, you would understand then and only then why we are so offended at your actions. . . . we all have a free will to choose. I'll be praying for your very soul.

So, all we ask, Mr. Wasserman, is that you reconsider your choice and of the blunder you are making and of the judgment you are heaving [sic] upon your own head.

Sincerely in love,

R. E. L.

Perfectly typed, grammatically perfect, two page letter on law firm letterhead to Mr. Jack Valenti copied to the heads of six Hollywood studios:

Re: "The Last Temptation of Christ"

Dear Mr. Valenti:

I have seen newspaper reports regarding a

statement you may have recently issued attacking "prior censorship" of "The Last Temptation of Christ." It was reported that your statement said "the key issue, the only issue is whether or not self-appointed groups can prevent a film from being exhibited to the public, or a book from being published, or a piece of art from being shown" and that you went on to say that you support Universal's "absolute right to offer to the people whatever movie it chooses."

I agree 100% with your statement that Universal has the right to produce and distribute any film that it wants to. However, I believe that you have misinterpreted the many people, like myself, who have written Universal to express our feelings about this film. Most people like me are not censors, do not want to be censors, and it is unfair for you to brand them with that name just because you disagree with their opinion. I want to make it very clear that I am not trying to censor anything Universal is doing, and I do not believe that most of the other people, like Dr. James Dobson and Dr. Bill Bright and Dr. Larry Poland, are trying to be censors. We are only expressing our heartfelt opinion about a business decision that Universal has apparently made . . . .

It appears to be the standard operating procedure of anyone in your industry to attack those who disagree with you by calling them names like "censor" or "fundamentalist" and to dismiss them as a fanatical, right-wing, fringe group. That name-calling response is just as immature now as when we were children, and misses the point entirely, which is that we are deeply hurt that someone would produce a film that tells the world that the man we love is a liar and a fool, and the religion we ascribe to is based on falsehoods. In fact, this film is contrary to all reliable historical evidence of Jesus' life and is being produced and distributed despite the fact that the producer knows it will offend millions of people. Why Universal chooses to purposely offend us, I don't know, but I do know they have made a conscious decision to go ahead in spite of the fact they fully understand how offensive the film is to those of us who love and believe in Jesus Christ. This is what we are upset about. We are not censors, we are just Christians,

Sincerely,

J. W. C., Jr.

Nicely hand written, three page letter from Las Vegas, Nevada:

Mr. Wasserman:

Earlier this week . . . it was brought to our attention that there is a movie currently in production to be aired this fall. The movie: "The Last Temptation of Christ." Well, without being judgmental, I was appalled. They read some of the excerpts of the book to us.

Sir, it's bad enough someone had no scruples

when writing this. With all the controversy already about religions and denominations, you would think Universal wouldn't want to stir up major problems . . . . If I had the money, power, or whatever it would take, I would stop this production. With all the evidence we do have of Christ's existence, you would think this novelist could have come up with a better portrayal of Christ's temptations, don't you agree? I pray to my savior and beg of you to stop this production before its too late . . . .

I realize movie making is a complicated matter and not exactly that easy for you maybe to just say, "Okay, we'll stop the movie." But could you find it in your heart to do what you can to put out the trash? All Christian institutions and people (true Christians) I'm sure would support you to the end, as they would their savior.

Thank you.

Sincerely concerned for the moral welfare of our country and our children--they are our future,

S. J.

A short, nicely typed letter from Greenville, Kentucky:

Dear Mr. Tom Pollock, Chairman of the Board, Universal Studio:

PLEASE DO NOT release the movie, "The Last

Temptation of Christ." It's breaking my heart to think someone would write a book like this.

And now, even worse, you want to make it a money movie.

When they say, "Money is the root of all evil," they're right . . . . PLEASE reconsider and DO NOT RELEASE this movie. I shall be praying for you. Don't become another Judas, and betray your Lord.

My prayers are with you, God help you.

P. G.

Three uncorrected letters from a fourth grade class in South Carolina:

Dear Universal Studios:

I am a Christian. I don't impprove with your new movie, "The Last Temtation of Christ." Because it tells people that he sined, but the Bible saids that God never sined. And that is a fact!

In Christ,

Joshua M.

Dear Universal Studios:

I am writing to you because I do not like your movie, "The Last Temptation of Christ"! I believe that the Lord <u>never sinned</u>!! I do not believe in spending 9 million dollars on a movie that is not true! You could be feeding the poor with that money. I'm sorry but I cannot come to your movie and I will tell others not to come. Please believe what I said about Jesus not sinning. If you want to know any more about Christ I left my return address.

Sincerely,

Melissa

Dear Universal:

I don't like the Idea of that movie called The Last temptation of Christ. I think it is wrong to God. I wrote this letter even if I don't know you it will make me sad even to my friends.

Sincerely,

Andrew

Just ten letters that fell into our hands from millions of responses--educated people, uneducated people, articulate people, inarticulate people, passionate people, restrained people, reasonable people, unreasonable people. But they were *people!* Real, live, thinking, hurting *people*.

They were *people* like the thousands who stimulated U.S. Congressmen Robert K. Dornan, William E. Dannemeyer, and Clyde C. Holloway to introduce House

Resolution 517 into the legislature "expressing the sense of the House that Universal Studios cancel the release of *The Last Temptation of Christ* . . ." and call on people to boycott them if they do release it. They were *people* like the constituents of Bo Boulter of Texas, Dan Burton of Indiana, Jack Davis of Illinois, Bill Hefner of North Carolina, Romano Mazzoli and Carroll Hubbard of Kentucky, Tom Lewis of Florida, Harold Volkmer of Missouri, Chris Smith of New Jersey, Gerald Solomon of New York, and Trent Lott and Sonny Montgomery of Mississippi who are among the growing number of congressmen agreeing to sponsor HR 517.

They were *people* like Archbishop Marcel Lefebvre who protested in St. Mark's square in Venice, Italy. They were *people* like Cardinal Albert Decourtray, archbishop of Lyon, France, and Jean-Marie Lustiger, Archbishop of Paris who opposed the film because it was "a wound to the spiritual liberty of millions of men and women."[48] They were *people* like Rev. Dr. William Oddie of the Church of England, who was offended by the film's theology, and Archbishop of Canterbury Robert Runcie who urged people to boycott it. They were *people* like the three in Pittsburgh who sued to have the title changed to *"The Lies and Profanations of Universal Pictures as Pertaining to the Life or Our Lord and Savior, Jesus Christ."*

MCA, Universal, and Cineplex Odeon didn't care about people *before* August 12-- We don't care about your [135,000 signatures on] petitions; leave them with the guards and we'll put them in the dump." Lew Wasserman, Sid Sheinberg, Tom Pollock, and Company haven't cared *since.* They are *still* so intent on rubbing this film in Christians faces that in mid-September they published 200,000 full color, eight page "discussion guides" for the film and sent them to churches, schools and other institutions! The guide hides the fact that Universal is the publisher, fails to quote one Bible verse, directs the reader to mostly non-Christian philosophers for answers, and presents the New Age philosophy of the film. In quoting Kazantzakis, the guide includes a long paragraph omitting only one radical phrase made by Nikos, " . . . I *became* Christ . . ."

It is clear that Universal leaders have not given one milligram of weight to the pleas of millions. They have obviously not cared whether they injured man or God --haven't cared if they created a *universal* offense.

12

The Last Temptation of Hollywood

> . . . Forgive us our debts, as we also have forgiven our debtors. And lead us not into temptation, but deliver us from evil . . .
>
> Matthew 6:12-13 NIV

The war over *The Last Temptation of Christ* was a shocker to Hollywood. It was a shocker because most film and TV professionals are out of touch with the basic values and thought patterns of middle America-- I don't mean "middle" geographically but "middle" morally. But it was also a shocker to Filmland, because Hollywood is accustomed to dealing with the video generation. The video generation--to say the least-- is not marked by taking firm stands on moral issues!

When I entered higher education in 1961, I remember the relish with which students in my college classes in sociology, family, logic, economics, and speech entered into the spirited, but well-motivated, debates in the classroom and in the student union. I will never forget the delight my classes demonstrated when I would intentionally take an unpopular position they knew I didn't hold--Marxism, atheism, slave ownership, existentialism, the abolition of marriage, the existence of UFO's--and defend it vigorously, daring them to put me to flight with superior evidence and argument. On occasions, some in the class would become so involved in the interchange that they would scream or weep. When I made a particularly convincing defense of a position, some would struggle thereafter, wondering if I *really was* a closet Marxist, atheist, or UFO freak.

Something frightening has happened to our culture in the last quarter of a century. I find high school and college age students, the video generation, less willing to fight for what they believe, less able to separate objective evidence from subjective experience, even deeply uncomfortable by the inevitable tension that is created by intellectual and verbal conflict. It seems that the only people who engage in an active defense of their beliefs are those at the extremes, at the far poles of issues. Thus, we observe the "Morton Downey, Jr., syndrome"--dialogue without restraint, argument without evidence, and passion without compassion. This provides a vicarious thrill for the couch potatoes of America not unlike professional wrestling. Despite the fact that the world is won and lost over ideas, these ideological orgies of extremism aren't taken too seriously; it's *theater*.

Hollywood was also shocked because of *who* the opponent was in the LTOC conflict--Christians! Certainly some of the *last* people the media would expect to engage in strong debate are Christians--at least Christians of anything but the "extremist" variety. So-called "mainline" Christian leadership has become so immersed in the values of the culture that it has abandoned many prime values of its faith. So, much of the laity has been swallowing full and free divorce and remarriage, gay priests, sexual liberation, situational ethics, and the death of absolutes. These values have often been spoon fed to them by "clergy" who are products of seminaries without moral walls.

224

In fact, the Christian community has largely joined the pagans in espousing a prime value of American culture which lies at the heart of media othodoxy--"openness." "Keeping your options open" is dogma in Medialand, despite the fact that no life can be lived successfully on this guiding premise. I once saw a rather profound statement on a picket sign at a porno house protest: "Some minds are so open they should be closed for repairs."

I would be the first to recognize that the concept of original sin doesn't "play well" in media. Undeniably, the same "gravitational pull" that draws you into overeating, alcoholism, sexual addiction, indolence, deceit, and infidelity is operational in Tinseltown. But rather than *fighting* the law of entropy in values, Hollywood has *merchandised* it! Take a serious look at the movie ads in today's paper or the promos for upcoming adventure programs on TV--they *feature* wrongdoing! Norman Lear, addressing professional peers years ago, set forth the premise that for a story to be commercially successful in Hollywood it has to break at least three of the ten commandments! One of Filmtown's big time producers in the fifties said sex is what sells. He explained that that was why Jane Russell was so hot at the box office and Lassie was on television. That was before Jane had her life changed by Jesus Christ and there was as much or more money to be made on TV as in films.

Day after day, week after week, Hollywood plays with the temptation to profit from sleaze. Before Metromedia, now the Fox TV network, was bought by Ruppert Murdoch and began a kind of "yellow journalism of the airwaves," I would stop by periodically and chat with my friend Don, Channel 11's program manager and a man of considerable integrity. One day he told me of Metromedia's struggle with temptation.

"Larry," he said, "let me give you an example of the kind of issues we face. As you may know, evening news is a major focal point of our programming. Every station wants to draw viewers to its news programming because it is a heavily watched hour and it gives you the ability to "shoehorn" the viewer into your prime time fare. Recently we have been losing out in the news ratings to other stations in town who are putting sexually titillating material into their news hours."

My mind raced across a number of promos I had seen for newstime features like, "The Latest Lingerie from the Playboy Mansion," "Hollywood's Sexiest Men," "Nude Beaches of the World," "The Year's Most Daring Swimsuits," or "A Look into the World of Male Strippers." I was beginning to understand.

"We don't want to do that kind of programming," Don continued, "But we can track the numbers, and there is no denying that those features are whipping us in the ratings. So, after the producer and management agonized over it, we have started doing some of the same stuff on our *P. M. Magazine* show."

They yielded to temptation. They took one more nibble on the apple. Now, under the Fox ownership, Channel 11 is putting out titillation as more or less common fare.

This has been the progression in Hollywood's Garden of Eden. For decades TV and movies producers have been progressively seduced by the forbidden fruit. They

226

were teased by its attractiveness--and *yielded* by featuring the short skirts and tight sweaters of the fifties. They held back the leaves to see the apple more clearly--and *yielded* to the nudity of the Playboy generation, the sixties. They listened to the lies of the Serpent denouncing God's words--and *yielded* to blatant attacks on absolute morality in the seventies. They touched and fondled the fruit--and *yielded* to the porno film flood of the eighties. Hollywood's Eve,with some residual naivete, bit into the fruit--and, having yielded, turned morally condemned practices into public spectacles, orgies, parades--even "pride."

But in 1988 Filmland's first man ate the fruit. In 1988, with full knowledge and premeditation, Adam exposed his nakedness at MCA/Universal and Cineplex Odeon. He took a big bite out of the produce of the Tree of the Knowledge of Good and Evil. He agreed to take on a film that he knew from observing the fate of Eve would push his world beyond the limits of God's gracious restraints.

The proof that Hollywood's Adam ate the apple is in the fig leaves he used to try to hide his offenses: Hush, hush shootings in Morocco. Stonewalled entertainment reporters in Los Angeles. Hired Christian "decoys" in Universal City. Quickly retracted scripts in Burbank. Secret screenings for insiders in New York. A matrix of lies and deceptions to the voices of reverence in . . . Lynchburg, Virginia . . . Tupelo, Mississippi . . . Pomona, California . . . Arrowhead Springs, California . . . Nashville, Tennessee . . . Charlotte, North Carolina . . . Gower Street in Hollywood . . . Van Nuys Boulevard in Van Nuys . . . Sacramento, California . . . Washington, D.C. . . . Birmingham, Alabama . . . London, England . . . Venice, Italy . . . Calcutta, India . . . and the

Vatican in Rome.

To paraphrase the words of Filmtown's "holy writ," *Daily Variety*, "even if the wrath of God does not fall on Universal, the wrath of God's well organized, media savvy armies *must!*" If, as Pat Buchanan postulated, Hollywood has said, "Hey, you Christians, look here; we're showing your God and Savior, Jesus Christ, having sex with Mary Magdalene; now, what are you going to do about it?" We jolly well better do something about it!

Why had we better?

This was not "just a movie" any more than the flag is "just a piece of cloth" or a diploma is "just a piece of paper." To say that this intentional and conspiratorial attack on the Christian community over many months by Universal City's toughest was "just a movie" and "What's the big deal; our God isn't threatened" is to say that the bombing of Pearl Harbor was just a "prank" and "What's the big deal; God doesn't care who wins wars." This *Last Temptation* decision, backed by the billions of a major U. S. corporation, and supported by a gaggle of creative leftists in Movie City *is without precedent in the two hundred year history of our nation and the 75 year history of the film business!* This is a symbol of a new era of Christ-smearing and Christian bashing in our culture--an era that is here to stay unless decent, moral people everywhere get off their duffs, take action, and speak up.

Temptation was not a first for the entertainment business, just *the highest order of offense* and *the most public assault* on Christ and Judeo-Christian values *by a major corporation*. That is what sets it apart.

This kind of assault has been going on under cover of journalistic darkness in Hollywood for years. In nearly nine years of working quietly with top people of faith inside film and television, I have heard many stories about this kind of assault. It is the writer who has only two paragraphs of his movie-of-the-week script cut out, the two paragraphs in which the key figures in the story pray, speak of Christ, or espouse the Christian faith. It is the TV co-host who is ordered off the set by the show producer because he will not consume an alcholic beverage on camera. It is the soap actress who is fired because she will not engage in sexual conduct as part of her role. It is the dancer who loses her job because she will not dance sexually suggestive routines on a prime time dance show. It is the actress who is out of work for refusing to grant sexual favors to the show's producer or executive. It is the noted character actor who is out of the business today because the "heavy" roles were all requiring him to use language off the restroom wall. Every one of these illustrations is backed by a real life story to which I cannot put names for the protection of those involved.

Within a few days of the release of *Temptation*, I received a letter from Tom, a "struggling Christian actor" who relayed the following story:

> I was glancing through the show section of *The Orange County Register* a few weekends ago and couldn't help feeling . . . anger and frustration. In the same section that contained a rave review of the blasphemous "Last Temptation of Christ" was a casting notice for a play entitled, "Fanmail for Psonic Truth from Fanatic Christians with Bombs and

229

Bibles." The title speaks volumes. I was outraged but decided to audition as a means of finding out about the play . . . just the same old Christian-bashing garbage we are used to. The glorification of sex and drugs, the non-stop use of language straight from the bathroom wall. And worst of all . . . the portrayal of Christians as fanatical zealots for standing against these things.

Along with the usual targets for Christian bashers, i. e. Swaggart and Baker, the dialogue contained putdowns of your group, Mastermedia. I was outraged! Enough is enough! Jesus saved me from a life of drugs and crime. If it wasn't for Jesus I would probably be dead by now. Through His love I turned my life around and discovered acting. It hurts me to see a movie that portrays Him as a lustful wimp. It hurts even more to see a play that portrays me as a fanatic for feeling this way about my Savior. . .

Some time ago a female co-worker and I were providing counsel and encouragement to a key lady executive in one of the biggest studios in town and ended up eyewitnesses to the following crime. The lady executive held a "co-director" position in the television division of the studio with a man who was homosexual. He had had a live-in lover for decades and, further, showed tremendous contempt for the Christian faith. This man, who functioned more like a "boss" than a co-director, was into occult types of religious experience. The executive, a sensitive and growing Christian, had quietly sought out support and Christian fellowship from her female co-workers who were Christians--on lunch hours and away from work.

Before leaving for some much needed vacation time, the lady approached her boss and outlined her holiday plans. She included details of a trip to Virginia to be on a Christian talk show. With no apparent negative response from her boss, she suspected nothing. Was she wrong!

Within a few days of her return she was summarily dismissed without adequate explanation. Her office possessions were put in boxes and set outside the office door, and skant financial provision was given for her severance. It settled out that her boss had apparently watched the show, was enraged at her open profession of her Christian faith, and especially of what he perceived to be the "proselyting" of other employees.

I was so enraged at the injustice that, without the executive's knowledge or permission, I called the president of that studio division, one of the ten most powerful men in film and TV, and told him the story. His curt and defensive response was "We don't give a damn what anybody believes around here." But we later learned that the studio did prepare itself for a wrongful dismissal suit, which alternative the lady chose not to pursue.

I say this not to portray that this kind of discrimination is *typical* of Hollywood. Thank God, it isn't! But the fact that it happens *at all* and that it is happening with increasing frequency is an ominous sign of increasing Christian bashing.

I deeply believe that the lives of two wonderful people,

singer Anita Bryant and her ex-husband, Bob Green, were nearly destroyed by the violence of Christian bashing of the most extreme form. I remember the touching moment Bob and I had at a convention during the overwhelming attacks against Anita for her expression of her Christian convictions against homosexuality. Bob told of the constant harassment by the gay community. He described the threats, the bomb scares at her concerts, the vitriolic attacks by the press, and the emotional toll it was taking on their lives and marriage. He told of the blackballing of Anita in the industry and of the increasing destruction of her career. With tears he said, "Larry, I never asked for this!"

In this free society those two shouldn't have *received* it either! Righteous, decent people all over America should have risen to defend their rights to proclaim their convictions and should have denounced the violence of their enemies. People inside the gay and lesbian community who are familiar with "gay bashing" techniques should have spoken up in their defense. Civil libertarians should have been leading the charge! The American *Civil Liberties* Union should have been engaging in its usual legal terrorism to stop the discriminatory nonsense. But, where Anita Bryant and Bob Green were concerned, First Amendment freedoms were for "the other guys."

Most conservative Christians would get a better shake from Hollywood if they were from a favored minority like native Americans. After all, Steven Spielberg changed his plans to shoot a picture on Hopi Indian territory when he received a complaint suggesting he would be violating the sacred land of the Hopis. And CBS television altered the content of a "Peanuts" cartoon show about Thanksgiving to remove reference to American Indians as "savages" when a native American group complained.

I can tell you of the violent responses and discrimination my family and I have received on two prior occasions when I have taken unpopular moral stands in public. I can tell you of being called every name in the book, of being threatened and harassed in the middle of the night, of having close, Christian friends turn cold because they believed the "half stories" the media put out to discredit me. I am not whining, and I don't view those experiences with a "suffering for Jesus" martyr spirit, either. But I am telling you the violence against faith and moral absolutes is getting *worse!*

The Last Temptation is the out-from-under-the-covers expression of a growing and vicious attempt to silence all voices of reverence for Christ, limits on conduct, traditional family values, and basic national morality. If you don't believe it, watch for the reaction to this book. Listen for the "voices of free speech, academic freedom, First Amendment rights, creative license, and artistic liberty" turn strangely silent or violent at my attempt to meet them on their own turf.

Just a few days before I penned this, I got a clipping from the August 25,1988, *Columbus* (Ohio) *Dispatch.* Syndicated columnist Mary Anne Dolan viciously attacked Donald Wildmon and Christians. Ms. Dolan talked about *Last Temptation's* receiving " . . . the hoped-for boost from publicity fostered by the reverend Donald Wildmon and his pack of howling censors." She manipulated the facts to create the false impression that he and "two Christian evangelists in

Southern California" gathered "a 25,000 person protest at Universal Studios to make his point. Crowds gathered *at their request outside the home of Universal chief Lew Wasserman, making blatant anti-Jewish claims* [emphasis added]."

In a biting projection of her own bitterness, Mary Anne says:

> Some will feel the zing of scarcastic humor coming over them when they see the movie and hear Willem Dafoe, who plays Christ, say to his Judas, 'I see men and I feel sorry for them, that's all.' *They will be thinking of Wildmon . . .* what needs to be said of Wildmon is that he gives opportunism and self-gratification a new name: *religion.* [emphasis added].

I have no problem with Ms. Dolan's use of sharp words. I have used a few myself. I do have a problem with the inaccuracy which results in her falsifying the facts of the protest. And I really do have a problem with the unmistakable intent of her last sentence. For Mary Anne Dolan it's apparent that the enemy is *religion.*

An editorial in the *Orange County* (California)*Register*, by Bob Emmers pours more acid on believers, referred to as Those Who Know Better:

> Let's suppose for a minute that the movie is more or less blasphemous, whatever that means.
>
> Let's suppose the movie does portray Christ as a sex-starved lout, as some of Those Who Know Better charge. Let's suppose the movie does

234

mock Jesus. Let's suppose the movie does raise questions about whether Jesus is the son of God. Let's suppose the movie does contain, gasp, sex and nudity. Let's suppose all of this is true.

So what?

I still ought to be able to go see it without a bunch of holier-than-thou twits telling me it's not good for me.

After all, one man's blasphemy is another man's piety, and the Constitution protects it all.

The problem with Those Who Know Better is that they actually think they do . . .[49]

Or how about this column from the *Detroit Free Press* by Mike Duffy?

They're back. The know-nothings have found a new cause. They always do.

This time, they're raising a ruckus over *"The Last Temptation of Christ"* . . . . The American ignoramous faction is perpetually geeked up on self-righteous bile. It always needs fresh meat. Fresh meat and fear. Fresh meat and intolerance.

And this time? Fresh meat and censorship. Bring us the head of Martin Scorsese . . . . They do so enjoy dishing out their own special brand of yahoo demagoguery.

It must be nice to have a monopoly on the truth.

I'm puzzled. How is it some of these people who call themselves fundamentalist Christians can spew such fundamentally un-Christian hatred?

And let's make no mistake, hatred and intolerance are exactly what we're talking about here . . . .

Anti-intellectual, anti-freedom of speech, anti-Semitic, you name it and there are some know-nothings who practice it.

They looked for Reds under every bed with Joe McCarthy.

They cheered police dogs in Selma . . . .

And now the know-nothing wacky pack has latched onto Martin Scorsese and "The Last Temptation of Christ."

Freedom of choice? They prefer to trample the very notion.

Being a know-nothing means never having to live in the real world.

These sour, fun-loathing people are experts at wrapping themselves in flags and Bibles, while pandering to exaggerated notions of patriotism and piety.

And once again, they have been blinded by

the dark light of their own sanctimonious blather. . . .[50]

If you are a sensitive believer in Christ and one of the millions who expressed themselves regarding LTOC, how does it make you feel to be characterized as "a pack of howling censors," "Those Who Know Better," "know nothings," and "a bunch of holier-than-thou twits"? Does it feel good being called fun-loathing, anti-intellectual, anti-semitic yahoos "geeked up on self-righteous bile"? Do you like being accused of cheering police dogs in Selma or looking for Reds under every bed with Joe McCarthy?

The era of Christian bashing is here and is in full swing. If you think for a minute that you can put down this book, escape into that 21 inch drain pipe into your living room, and hide from the increasing hostility and impending persecution coming your way, forget it. There will be no escaping.

My friend, if you care one whit about this great country, about the freedom of religion that this republic has provided for two centuries, about faith in Jesus Christ or, for that matter, faith of *any* variety, the time has come to speak up and stand up. As Joseph Farah, editor of the *Glendale News-Press,* put it:

> In fact, if Christians don't take an all-out stand against the release of this film, they will never again be taken seriously as an interest group. If Universal Studios and its parent company, MCA, are not made to pay dearly for their role in producing and distributing the movie, the media will know that a permanent 'open season' on Christians has been declared.

Would MCA and Universal risk a nationwide boycott against all of its lucrative properties for the sake of one box-office smash? If so, for Christians there will be no backing down from such a dare.[51]

Christian, you can take little comfort in the fact that 78% of Americans say Jesus is God or the Son of God. It matters little that 66% of America say that they have "made a commitment to Christ." If that commitment is not translated into *open declaration* and *active participation* in our society, this nation will stew in its own secularistic juices. Every excuse you use for keeping silent will become your epitaph. Every rationalization you set forth to justify your refusal, actively and sacrificially, to defend your Lord, defend your faith, or defend faith in general will be carved on your tombstone. It will be chiseled there by the people in this society who have succumbed to the last temptation there is--the temptation to defy God himself and His people.

Do and say nothing and we will be driven out of the Garden with those who took the first bite!

Before his death at the hands of the Nazis, Martin Niemoller, the German Lutheran pastor wrote:

> In Germany when they came for the Communists, I didn't speak up because I was not Communist. Then they came for the Jews, and I did not speak up because I was not a Jew. Then they came for the trade unionists, and I did not speak up because I wasn't a trade unionist. Then they came for the Catholics, and I was a Protestant, so I didn't speak up. Then

they came for me . . . by that time there was no one to speak up for anyone.[52]

In the words of the first century apostles of Jesus Christ when ordered by the authorities to shut up, "We *cannot but speak* the things we have seen and heard."

Keep silent and you will succumb to *The Last Temptation of Christendom*.

Appendix

A. Kazantzakis: The Mind Behind the Movie

By Robert M. "Buster" Holmes, Jr.

To understand the Jesus character presented in the movie directed by Martin Scorsese, it is helpful to learn more about Nikos Kazantzakis, author of the original novel, *The Last Temptation of Christ*. A few brief, but telling, excerpts from various writings reveal Kazantzakis' perverted picture of Christ and his true objective in producing this work.

1.

In *Nikos Kazantzakis, A Biography Based On His Letters* (Simon and Schuster, 1968), his wife, Helen Kazantzakis, documents two of many letters which her husband sent to his Swedish friend and translator, Borje Knos. These letters reveal Nikos Kazantzakis' true intentions in writing *The Last Temptation of Christ*.

> I wanted to renew and supplement the sacred Myth that underlies the great Christian civilization of the West. It isn't a simple 'Life of Christ'. It's a laborious, sacred, creative endeavor to reincarnate the essence of Christ, setting aside the dross--falsehoods and pettinesses which all the churches and all the cassocked representatives of Christianity have heaped upon His figure, thereby distorting it.

The pages of my manuscript were often smudged because I could not hold back my tears. Parables which Christ could not possibly have left as the Gospels relate them, I have supplemented, and I have given them the noble and compassionate ending befitting Christ's heart. Words which we do not know that He said I have put into His mouth because He would have said them if His Disciples had had His spiritual force and purity. (505-506)

I'm glad you liked The Last Temptation . . . Here in Holland, I have had some interesting conversations with pastors about the theological side of the work. Some were shocked that Christ had temptations. But while I was writing this book, I felt what Christ felt. I became Christ. And I know definitely that great temptations, extremely enchanting and often legitimate ones, came to hinder him on his road to Golgotha. But how could the theologians know all this? (515-516)

In the same book Mrs. Kazantzakis states the real motive behind Kazantzakis' writings in *The Last Temptation of Christ* and *The Saviors of God: Spiritual Exercises.*

To found a religion, to found a religion at all costs, this was the obsession haunting Kazantzakis over a long span of years . . . After harsh struggles, he came to realize and know that the 'new myth' had escaped him. (61)

2.

Kimon Friar, Kazantzakis' friend and translator of Kazantzakis' book *The Saviors of God: Spiritual Exercises*, makes the following observations about Kazantzakis' beliefs in that book's introduction (Simon and Schuster, 1968).

He struggled, therefore, with the only tools he had, pen and paper, striving to purify his style, dreaming of a new theology, a new religion of political action in which the dogmatic, teleological God of the Christians would be dethroned to be replaced by dedication to an evolutionary and spiritual refinement of matter. (16)

He rejected the materialistic bias of communism, but similarly rejected the dogmatic and anthropomorphic God of the Christians as equally materialistic. God, for Kazantzakis, was not an already predetermined goal toward which men proceed, but a spirituality ceaselessly and progressively created by nature as it evolves toward greater and higher refinement. (20)

Bergson and Nietzsche must stand as the two main streams of Kazantzakis' philosophical thought . . . who helped him conclude that God is not a teleology, not an entelechy, not a predetermined Father, Son, or Holy Ghost who aids man in the salvation of his soul . . . (38)

3.

In *The Saviors of God: Spiritual Exercises* , Kazantzakis wrote in the chapter entitled "The Relationship Between God and Man":

My God is not All-holy. He is full of cruelty and savage justice, and he chooses the best mercilessly. He is without compassion; he does not trouble himself about men or animals; nor does he care for virtues and ideas. He loves all these things for a moment, then smashes them eternally and passes on. (Verse 31)

My God is not All-knowing. His brain is a tangled skein of light and darkness which he strives to unravel in the labyrinth of the flesh. (Verse 33)

It is not God who will save us--it is we who will save God, by battling, by creating, and by transmuting matter into spirit. (Verse 47)

4.

Finally, from *Nikos Kazantzakis: A Biography Based On His Letters* , Kazantzakis discusses his play, *Sodom and Gomorrah*, and his book, *The Last Temptation* :

Oh how I've toppled and buffeted Abraham and his beard! And how I've raised and sanctified Judas Iscariot right alongside Jesus in this book I'm writing now. For anyone who creates, all these saintly or diabolical Gestalten [forms] are but pawns for the supreme game . . . I found a different Abraham in the Bible. So, just the way astute photographers do, I retouched him to make him serve my purposes. It's simple; and so good and just to topple tradition a bit . . . For the creator, just and unjust, good and evil, God and Devil no longer exist. There is only the hungry flame devouring all these succulent foods. And the devil's flesh is always more nourishing than God's. And I love it, provided that it is consumed, digested, and assimilated . . . (477)

B. How Bad is the Film?

By Robert M. "Buster" Holmes, Jr.

Following are descriptions of some scenes that are particularly offensive to those who are committed to the biblical and historical view of Jesus of Nazareth. Inserted after certain scene descriptions are some comments made by people who supported the movie and belittled our concerns. These appraisals seem to us to be particularly incredible in light of the content which precedes them. Judge for yourself!

The scenes described are in the order presented in the movie. This material was constructed from the combined notes of four people who viewed the film. A number of Jesus' thoughts are included as "voice overs" marked "VO." Comments in brackets are the author's comments.

1.

The movie opens with the Jesus character lying on the ground, apparently in pain, suffering from a headache which he describes through a voice-over (VO). He says the feeling or nightmare is very tender and loving--at first. Then the pain begins, like claws ripping and tearing under his skin.

Then he awakens. Another VO follows in which Jesus explains:
"First I fasted for three months. I even whipped myself before I went to sleep. At first it worked, then the pain came back . . ."

2.

In a scene where Judas has caught Jesus making crosses which are used by the Romans to execute Jewish zealots, Judas berates Jesus by calling him a disgrace and a coward. He asks Jesus how he will ever pay for his sins, and Jesus replies:
"With my life . . ."
[Jesus sins and has to die for his own misdeeds?]

Judas, in his frustration, pushes down the cross-piece Jesus has been working on, then pushes and shakes Jesus around the shop. At one point Jesus falls to his knees and kisses Judas on the hand.
Judas demands:
"Give your life? What do you mean?"
Jesus:
"Please. . . I don't know. I don't know . . . I'm struggling."
Judas:
"I struggle. You collaborate."

"The inner struggle . . . really resonated with me. When I was a pastor, I preached that. I felt Jesus really did have those struggles." (Robert Maddox, Americans United for Separation of Church and State, "Some Clerics See No Evil in 'Temptation,'" *Los Angeles Times***)**

3.

As Jesus carries the cross-piece to the execution site, villagers mock him, children throw rocks at him, Mary Magdalene spits in his face, and then Jesus assists the Roman soldiers who nail the Jewish zealot to the cross. As blood from the zealot's nail wounds spurts into his face, Jesus begins to think to himself:
"God loves me. I know He loves me. I want Him to stop . . . I want Him to hate me . . . I want Him to find somebody else.

245

I want to crucify every one of His messiahs."

As Jesus is thinking the above, the scene shifts to his shop where he is seen later that night writhing on the floor, apparently from another "attack."

"The movie is artistically excellent and theologically sound . . . Christ is presented as a muscular, strong, manly person who sweated, bled, had doubts and was, as the Bible says, 'tempted in every way yet without sin." (Rev. Paul Moore, Episcopal Bishop of New York, "Religious Leaders Happy With Movie," N.Y. Times News Service)

4.

As Jesus and his mother talk, Mary asks if he is sure the headaches and the voices that plague him are from God, because, if its the devil, the devil could be cast out. [Mary thinks Jesus might be demon possessed?]

Jesus responds that he isn't sure of anything, and then asks:
"But what if it's God? You can't cast out God can you?"

"MARTIN SCORSESE, AMERICA'S MOST GIFTED, MOST DARING MOVIEMAKER, MAY HAVE CREATED HIS MASTERPIECE. Willem Dafoe's spiky, ferocious, nearly heroic performance is a perfect servant to the role. He finds sense in Jesus' agonies; he finds passion in the parables." (Richard Corliss, *Time*)

5.

While Jesus walks alone by a lake, he hears footsteps, turns and asks who is following him via VO. Then he falls to the ground holding his head.

"Anyone for whom the story of Christ . . . has any resonance at all is likely to find this an exquisitely powerful film. The emotional charge is tremendous." (Bill Cosford, *The Miami Herald*)

6.

Jesus enters a village, meets a bare-breasted woman at a well (he says nothing), follows a man who he thinks is an angel to Mary Magdalene's brothel, then he sits with about 10 other men who watch Magdalene as she has sex with a customer behind a partial, transparent screen. Jesus sits and watches as all the men take their turn. [In the widely circulated script Jesus waited in the courtyard until all the men left. Why did Scorsese want Jesus inside . . . watching?]

When he alone remains, Jesus explains that he wants Magdalene to forgive him, because he has done many bad things, but the worst things he has done have been to her. [In the Kazantzakis novel, Jesus and Mary were betrothed, but Jesus wouldn't or couldn't go through with the marriage because of his "mission" in life, so Magdalene turned to prostitution.]

Magdalene tells Jesus that he is just like the other men, that he's pitiful, and she hates him . . . he's just clinging to God like he did his mother. She invites him to save her soul through sex. He pulls away.
Later she says:
"All I ever wanted was you."
Jesus:
"What do you think I wanted?"

"What I've tried to create is a Jesus who, in a sense, is just like any other guy in the street.

In his struggle to reach God and find God, he reflects all our struggles. I thought it would give us all hope." (Martin Scorsese, "In The Name of Jesus," *People Magazine*)

7.

Jesus and a monk talk on a hillside near a desert monastery where Jesus sought refuge. Jesus bemoans his lot in life and his sins:
"I'm a liar, a hypocrite. I'm afraid of everything. I don't ever tell the truth. I don't have the courage . . . I want to rebel against you, against everything, against God. But I'm afraid. You want to know who my mother and father are? You want to know who my god is--fear . . ."

When the monk interrupts that the more devils we have, the more chances we have to be cleansed, Jesus counters:
"Lucifer is inside me."

"The film will help people understand their own commitment to Jesus." (Rev. William Fore, National Council of Churches, *Time*)

8.

That night at the monastery, serpents coil out of the ground in Jesus' hut, and one speaks to Jesus in Magdalene's voice. Jesus tells the serpents to leave him and they disappear.

Then the monk appears and tells Jesus that he has been purified, because the snakes came from within him (Jesus). Now Jesus must leave, but he doesn't want to go, because he is not sure where he will go or to whom he will speak or what he will say.
The monk asks:
Do you love mankind?"
Jesus:

"I see men and I feel sorry for them. That's all."
Monk:
"That's enough."

9.

Later that night Judas appears at Jesus' hut. He is sent by
the zealots to execute Jesus. Jesus tells him to go ahead
because he doesn't want to fight God any more, and he's
ready to die because he has been purified. [Why would a
sinless Christ need purification?]

Judas decides not to kill Jesus, then demands to know
Jesus' secret -- what's behind the voices, the fainting, the
visions, and magic.
Jesus responds:
"Pity."
Judas:
"Pity for whom?   Yourself?"
Jesus:
"Pity for men . . . I feel pity for everything, donkeys,
grass, sparrows . . . Everything's a part of God."

Judas then asks Jesus if he is afraid of dying. Jesus
simply replies that death is a door that opens, and we just
enter.

**"To our discredit, many Christians have shown a
tendency to swallow and spread unfounded
rumors about supposed threats to our faith."
(Editorial, *United Methodist Reporter*)**

[No rumors here; just Kazantzakis' twisted theology]

10.

On his way to give the Sermon on the Mount, Jesus is
concerned about whether he will say the right thing or the

wrong thing, since God has so many miracles. During the sermon, Jesus is asked to explain the seed in the parable of the sower.
Jesus:
"Love. Love one another."

Jesus then describes how he overcame his fear of God, who used to jump on his head like a wild bird with sharp claws: "But then one morning He came to me and blew over me like a cool breeze and said, 'Stand up.' And I said 'here I am.'"

"BRILLIANT, THRILLING AND PROFOUNDLY SPIRITUAL." **(Dennis Cunningham, CBS-TV)**

11.

Judas and Jesus talk in the evening after the Sermon on the Mount, which took place just after Jesus had stopped the stoning of Mary Magdalene. [Magdalene, in the movie, was the woman taken in adultery.]

Jesus:
"How could I be the Messiah? When those people were torturing Magdalene I wanted to kill them. When I opened my mouth, out came the word "love." Why? I don't understand."

Later, before they go to sleep, Jesus asks Judas to stay with him because he is afraid. [The King of kings and Lord of lords is afraid?] Judas consents and they sleep with Jesus resting on Judas' chest.

"It's just another interpretation in the same way that Matthew, Luke, and John are." **(Cathy Smith, producer for *Showtime* cable TV, "'I pray that it doesn't get ugly,'" *USA Today*)**

12.

Jesus sought out John the Baptist for confirmation of his messiahship. John was baptizing at the Jordan. There is wailing and full, frontal, female nudity. Proselytes are scraping themselves with stones.

Two times John the Baptist asks Jesus who he is, and then he asks Jesus if he is the Chosen One.
Jesus responds:
"I don't know. Tell me."

[John never acknowledges that Jesus is the Chosen One. There is no voice from the Father. There is no dove.]

13.

While in the desert alone, Jesus is startled when a column of fire appears in the night. Jesus thinks it is the Archangel. As they talk, the Archangel tells Jesus that he overheard him cry out to God when he was just a child saying:

"Make me God. God, make me God."
A little later Jesus realizes he is talking to Satan.

The column of fire disappears, but a small tree with lush apples appears right next to Jesus. Jesus picks one of the apples and takes a bite [like in the Garden of Eden?]. Blood pours from the apple and runs down Jesus' chin and chest. Then the voice of Satan calls out: "We will meet each other again."

"SUPERBLY CRAFTED FILMMAKING. Scorsese has created a work of immense imagination, one that never betrays its unshakable faith. . ." (Marshall Fine, Gannett News Service)

14.

Following Jesus' temptation in the wilderness, he needs help from Lazarus' sisters, Mary and Martha. After they nurse him back to health, he thanks them by saying: " . . . You took me in, fed me, restored me, and God came down and went into my heart." [Jesus isn't God yet?]

When Jesus returns to his disciples, he tells them to prepare for war. Then, while kneeling, he reaches into his belly and pulls out his bloody heart to offer it to his disciples:
"This is my heart. Take it. God is inside of us. The devil is outside us . . . We'll pick up an axe and cut the devil's throat . . ."
He put his heart back into his chest.
"I believed in love. Now I believe in this [Jesus holds up an ax] . . ."

"The movie does not even approach a truly radical interpretation of the life of Christ . . . It may well be one of the most doctrinaire visions of the life of Christ . . . so much so that without all the controversy, liberal critics might well have written it off as a 'Sunday-school movie'." (William Arnold, *The Seattle Post-Intelligencer*)

15.

Following the healing of demoniacs, Jesus meets a blind man. He mixes sand and spit and places it over the man's eyes. Then he kisses each eye as he speaks through a VO:
"Jeremiah, Moses, Elijah, Isaiah--touch my mouth, touch my lips." [What about God the Father?]

The man is healed.

"I thought there was a miracle included for

252

every fundamentalist around." (Rev. Eugene Schneider, public relations officer, United Church of Christ, "Some Clerics See No Evil in Temptation," *Los Angeles Times***)**

16.

A Sadducee confronted Mary Magdalene about entering the wedding at Cana because marriage is holy and Magadalene, a prostitute, is unholy. Jesus defended Magdalene by saying that Heaven is like a wedding and everyone is invited, because God's world is big enough for everybody.
Sadducee:
"Nazarene, that is against the Law."
Jesus:
"Then the Law is against my heart."

"I was not offended in any way Scripture was used and applied." (Rev. Charles Bergstrom, chairman, People For The American Way executive committee, former Washington lobbyist for the Lutherans, "Some Critics See No Evil in 'Temptation,' *Los Angeles Times***)**

17.

Just before zealots kill Lazarus, who is Jesus' greatest living miracle, they ask him some questions about being raised from the dead. A zealot asks:
"How do you feel?"
Lazarus (who doesn't know what the zealots are planning to do):
"I like the light."
The Zealots then wanted to know if life or death was better.
Lazarus:
"I was a little surprised. There isn't that much difference."

[No heaven and no hell?]

Then they kill Lazarus.

"IT IS WITHOUT QUESTION ONE OF THE MOST SERIOUS, LITERATE, COMPLEX, AND DEEPLY RELIGIOUS FILMS EVER MADE, brilliantly directed by Martin Scorsese." (David Ehrenstein, *Los Angeles Herald Examiner)*

18.

To complete God's plan of redemption, Jesus has to convince Judas, his best and strongest friend, to betray him. Judas doesn't want to do it.
Jesus:
". . . God gave me the easier job--to be crucified."

"This film for me is like A BRILLIANT METAPHOR. Scorsese has given us a very contemporary image of Jesus, torn between body and soul, whose triumph is ultimately one of the will." (David Ansen, *Newsweek*)

19.

During his agony on the cross Jesus has a dream. An angel in the form of a little girl of nine or ten takes Jesus down from the cross and explains that she is his Guardian Angel sent from God to save him from the cross. Then she leads him away from Golgotha into a beautiful land. Jesus asks if the beautiful land is the world of God. She explains it is earth:
"It hasn't changed, you have. You can now see its true beauty, harmony between the earth and the heart. That is the world of God . . ."

["Harmony between the earth and heart" is the world of

254

God?]

The angel leads Jesus to Magdalene who is already prepared for their wedding. Presumably after the ceremony, She tends his wounds, and they have sex on screen. When she is several months pregnant, God appears to her in a blinding light and kills her. When Jesus finds her dead in their little house he runs outside in a rage.

"DEEPLY FELT AND ULTIMATELY FAITH AFFIRMING. Scorsese has filled this film with images that won't be easily forgotten." (Joel Siegel, *"Good Morning, America,"* ABC-TV)

His guardian angel comforts him by explaining that Magdalene is now immortal, she died happy, and besides:
". . . There's only one woman in the world, one woman with many faces. When this one falls, the next one rises."

She explains that Magdalene died, but Mary, Lazarus' sister, is Magadalene with a different face. And this new Mary carries Jesus' greatest joy . . . his son. The angel leads Jesus to Lazarus' sisters and explains:
"Come with me . . . This is the way the savior comes, gradually, from embrace to embrace, from son to son . . ."
Jesus:
"I understand."

Jesus evidently marries Mary and has children by her and by Martha [the implication is either bigamy or adultery]. Jesus supports his family as the village carpenter.

"It reaffirms the power of the Gospel by examining Christ's life from a new, accessible perspective . . . for an audience willing to re-examine basic beliefs, in search of a fresh understanding of Jesus that is no less moving than the simple stories taught in childhood." (Frank Gabrenyo, "The Last Temptation of

255

Christo,"*The Columbus Dispatch*, Columbus, Ohio)

20.

Also in the dream, Jesus confronts the apostle Paul who is preaching the gospel of the resurrected Christ. Jesus becomes angry and tells Paul that if he doesn't shut up, he (Jesus) will tell everyone the truth -- that he didn't rise from the dead and that he is a simple carpenter with a family.

Paul responds:
"Their only hope is the Resurrected Jesus. I don't care whether you are Jesus or not. The Resurrected Jesus will save the world and that's what matters."
Jesus:
"Those are lies. You can't save the world."
Paul:
"I've created truth out of what people needed and believed. If I have to crucify you to save the world, then I'll crucify you. And if I have to -- resurrect you..."

"I firmly believe that we have made a motion picture which will serve as a reaffirmation of faith to members of the Christian community." (Martin Scorsese, "Scorsese's 'Temptation' Not Exactly By The Book," *USA Today*)

21.

The final scenes show the old Jesus dying in his house while Jerusalem is burning. His disciples come to see him and Judas begins to berate him because he, Jesus, didn't die on the cross and lead the revolution.

Jesus explains that the Guardian Angel told him that God had changed his mind. At that time the Guardian Angel (still in the form of a little girl) changes into a column of fire. It

256

is Satan. He says:
"Jesus, I told you we would meet again."

Jesus realizes he has been fooled all those years since he came down from the cross, so he crawls outside his house and cries out to God for forgiveness, begs for another chance to be the Messiah, begs for a chance to die for mankind.

"This film for me is like a prayer. It is my way of worshipping." (Martin Scorsese, "In The Name of Jesus," *People Magazine*)

22.

Suddenly, Jesus is back on the cross. He realizes it was all a dream. Then he happily dies because he has resisted the last temptation.

"It [the film] uses Jesus as a fictional character, a metaphor, to find, I hope, a stronger emotional truth . . . and make it more appreciated by us and make it more serious for today . . ." (Martin Scorsese, "Scorsese Defends 'Temptation,'" *Hollywood Reporter*)

[There is greater, stronger "emotional truth" than Jesus?]

Finally . . .

Perhaps the most incredible comment made during the past few months came from Amy E. Schwartz, a member of the *Washington Post* editorial page staff in a *Washington Post* special carried in the *Chicago Sun Times* on August 12, page 35. Ms. Schwartz feels Christians should thank Martin Scorsese and Universal Pictures for releasing *The Last Temptation of Christ.*

257

"The appearance of books, plays, and movies that take religion seriously, even if they take liberties with dogma, is a sign not of secularism and disdain, but of just their opposite. That Martin Scorsese wanted to make a movie about this deeply religious novel, and that Universal Pictures wants to distribute it, mean that these mainstream arts people, so often attacked by the religious right, think these powerful matters of faith are worth dreaming and talking and seeing movies about."

No thank you, Amy.
No thank you, Martin.
No thank you, Universal.

C.   Holding MCA and Universal Accountable

Many Americans of all beliefs have realized the flagrant attack on religious faith created by the action of MCA/Universal and Cineplex Odeon which jointly funded and released *The Last Temptation of Christ*. Christians in particular see the need to hold these companies responsible for their callous rejection of the pleas of millions not to release this film.

If you would like to share in this effort, note the addresses of individuals and offices to whom you can express your convictions and the business interests from which you can withhold patronage.

1. Communicate with . . .

* *MCA-Universal*, 100 Universal City Plaza Blvd., Universal City, CA 91608
* *MCA-Universal* headquarters phones: (818) 777-1000, 777-1263, 777-1293, 777-1263, 777-5888

* Lew Wasserman, *MCA* Chairman of the Board (above address)
* Sidney Sheinberg, *MCA* President (above address)
* Tom Pollock, Chairman of the Board, *Universal Pictures* (above address)

* *Cineplex Odeon* 1303 Yonge Street, Toronto,Ontario, M4T 2Y9, Canada (416) 323-6600, FAX # (416) 964-1400

* Garth Drabinsky, President and CEO, *Cineplex Odeon* (above address)

* Major *Cineplex Odeon* shareholders:
  Mrs. Sandra Diane Kolber, Cineplex Director, c/o Hon. Ernest L Kolber, 630 Dorchester Blvd. W., 32nd Floor, Montreal, PQ H3B 1X5, Canada
  Charles R. Bronfman, The Seagram Co., 1430 Peel St., Montreal, PQ H3A 1S9, Canada
  Edgar M. Bronfman, Joseph E. Seagram and Sons, 375 Park Avenue, New York, NY 10152
  (The Bronfmans are Cineplex Odeon's largest shareholders controlling 24.6% of the shares)

2. Do Not Patronize . . .

* *Universal Studios Tour*, Universal City, CA, (818) 508-5444 and *Universal Studios*, Orlando, Florida
* *MCA Records*, division of MCA

* *MCA Videos and Tapes*
* *USA Network* (Cable TV) 50% owned by MCA
* *Spencer Gift Stores* (MCA subsidiary) 1050 Black Horse Pike, Pleasantville, NJ 08332 (609) 645-3300
* *Cineplex Odeon Theaters* (shared cost of film's production, co-released the film, and screened the film across the U.S.)
* *E. T., The Extra-Terrestrial.* Do not buy or rent the videotape of this Universal film from which Universal expects to take in $250 million.

D. Footnotes

1. "Religion in America: Report No. 259," *The Gallup Report*, Princeton, NJ, April, 1987, 28.
2. "Religion in America: Report No. 259," *Ibid.*, 18.
3. "Religion in America: Report No. 259," *Ibid.*, 28.
4. "Religion in America: Report No. 259," *Ibid.*, 28.
5. "Profile of the Christian Marketplace," American Research Corporation, Newport Beach, CA, 1980, 7.
6. Motion Picture Association of America figures for 1987 via September 23, 1988, phone conversation with Ratings Department. Of 483 movies rated (movies are voluntarily submitted to MPAA), 11 were rated G, 102 were PG, 73 were PG-13, 295 were R, and 2 were X.
7. Telephone conversation between Scott Dugan of *The Hollywood Reporter* and Tim Penland.
8. Excerpts from a transcript of the address by Pope John Paul II to media luminaries on September 15, 1987, provided by the Communications Department of the Archdiocese of Los Angeles.
9. Cooper, James F., "Two Films that attack Traditional Belief," *Between the Lines*, Vol. 1 No. 8, 13.
10. Lichter, Lichter, and Rothman, "Hollywood and

America: The Odd Couple," *Public Opinion,* December/January, 1983, 23.

11. "Connecticut Mutual Life Report on American Values in the '80's: The Impact of Belief," Research and Forecasts, Inc., New York, NY, 1981, 214-215.

12. Dart, John, "Evangelicals Intensify Struggle to Stop Film," *Los Angeles Times,* July 12, 1988, Part VI, 1.

13. Dawes, Amy, "Universal Target of 'Last' Protests," *Daily Variety,* July 13, 1988, 1.

14. "Religious Leaders Happy with Movie," *Warsaw* (Indiana)*Times-Union,* July 15, 1988, Section 1, 4.

15. Dart, John, "Some Clerics See No Evil in 'Temptation,'" *Los Angeles Times,* July 14, 1988, Part VI, 11.

16. Dobson, James, *Focus on the Family Newsletter,* Pomona, California, September, 1988, 4.

17. Buchanan, Patrick, "Christian-bashing a Popular Indoor Sport in Hollywood," *Glendale News Press,* July 27, 1988, Sec. A, 9.

18. "Connecticut Mutual Life Report on American Values in the '80's: The Impact of Belief,"*op. cit.,* 201-245.

19. *NFD Journal,* Publication of American Family Association, Tupelo, Mississippi, March, 1986, 7.

20. Press statement released by the Motion Picture Association of America, July,1988.

21. Pryor, Thomas, *Daily Variety,* "'Temptation': The Ultimate Expression of Censorship," July 27, 1988, 6.

22. Stein, Ben, *The View From Sunset Boulevard,* Anchor Press/ Doubleday, Garden City, NY, 1980, 83.

23. Stein, Ben, *Ibid.,* 84.

24. Lichter, Lichter, and Rothman, "Hollywood and America: The Odd Couple," *Public Opinion,* December/January, 1983, 24.

25. Lichter, Lichter, and Rothman, *Ibid.,* 23.

26. Kazantzakis, Nikos, *The Last Temptation of Christ,* Simon and Schuster, New York, NY, 1960, "A Note

on the Author and His Use of Language," by P. A. Bien, 505.

27. Dallas-Damis, Athena G., "Kazantzakis," *McGraw Hill Encyclopedia of World Biography*, New York, NY, Vol. 6, 1973, 144-146.

28. Press release by Billy Graham Association communicated by telephone to Tim Penland.

29. Hayakawa, S. I., *Language In Thought and Action*, Harcourt Brace Jovanovich, Inc., New York, NY, 40-41.

30. Hayakawa, S. I., *Ibid.*, 41.

31. Pryor, Thomas, *Daily Variety*, "'Temptation': The Ultimate Expression of Censorship," July 27, 1988, 6.

32. A letter to the editor, *Daily Variety*, July 27, 1988, 21.

33. Grassi, Giovanni, "Italians React to 'Christ' Venice Screening," *The Hollywood Reporter*, August 5, 1988, 1.

34. Eller, Claudia, "Universal Not Tempted to Pull 'Christ' Despite Tide of Protest," *The Hollywood Reporter*, July 20, 1988, 1.

35. White, Gayle, "Planned Early Release of 'Last Temptation' Deepens Christian Anger," *Atlanta Journal and Constitution*, August 6, 1988, Sec. B, 1.

36. Buchanan, Patrick, "Christian-bashing a Popular Indoor Sport in Hollywood," *op. cit.*, 9.

37. Buchanan, Patrick, *Ibid.*, 9.

38. White, Gayle, *op. cit.*, 1.

39. Leo, John, "A Holy Furor," *Time*, August 15, 1988, 35.

40. Cooper, Steve, "'Temptation' a Picture of its Makers," *The San Bernardino Sun*, August 8, 1988, 1.

41. Cooper, Steve, *Ibid*, 1.

42. Cooper, Steve, *Ibid*, 1.

43. Byrge, Duane, "Last Temptation of Christ," *The Hollywood Reporter*, August 8, 1988, 8.

44. Dart, John, "Church Declares 'Last Temptation' Morally Offensive," *Los Angeles Times*, August 10, 1988, Part II, 3.

45. "Venice Festival Screens Scorsese's 'Last Temptation,'" *Los Angeles Times*, September 9, 1988, Part IV, 4.

46. Personal conversation between Pat Broeske of *Los Angeles Times*, and Tim Penland.

47. Undistributed videotape of protest rally at which Dr. Richard G. Lee spoke.

48. "Venice Festival Screens Scorsese's 'Last Temptation,'" *op. cit.*, 4.

49. Emmers, Bob, "Film on Jesus Tempts Group to Boycott," *Orange County Register*, July 15, 1988, Section B, 1.

50. Duffy, Mike, "Yahoos Create Unholy Row Over Film About Christ," *Detroit Free Press*, August 10, 1988,

51. Farah, Joseph, "Hollywood's Ultimate Temptation," *Between The Lines*, August 1988, Vol. 1 No. 7, 11.

52. Niemoller, Martin, Quoted in "The Conejo Caller," Vol. XVI, No. 23, September 14, 1988

E. Acknowledgments

With deepest gratitude I recognize:

Tim Penland	For faithfully sticking by me in the trenches.
"Buster" Holmes	For endless hours of research, editing, and proofreading.
Rick Coltman	For assistance at every point.
Bret Welshymer	For tending to the many details.
Ruth Ann Wright	For managing my "schedule crunch" caused by the protest.
Les Stobbe	For wise, professional counsel.
Larry Thompson	For dedication to excellence.
Trinity Church	For the prayers, support, and encouragement of the elders, staff, and congregation for their senior minister in a time of pressure and need.
Frank Poland	Who taught his son that God defends those who stand for what is right.
Donna Lynn	For faithfulness, support, and love in extravagant proportions.
The Family	Christian, Desiree, Cherish, Destiny , Chalet, and Valor-- for enduring a preoccupied dad for five months.
The Key Men	For wise counsel, earnest prayers, and solid commitment.
Christ, the King	The One who has given me something noble for which to live and something great for which to die.

Keep up with the Spiritual War in Film and Television!

If you have been intrigued by this story of dramatic conflict in media over faith, morality, responsibility, and freedom and would like to keep up with what is going on as Christians express themselves more openly in the media marketplace . . .

WRITE NOW for your FREE subscription to the *Mediator.*

This informative, provocative, and easy-to-read, bi-monthly publication provides insights, critical concerns, evidences of God at work, stories of the spiritual war, and points for prayer and action.

Yours for the asking!

- -

Please send me the *Mediator!*
Mastermedia, 2102 Palm, Highland, CA 92346

Name

Street Address and Apartment Number

City, State, and Zip